DAVID ROBINSON

By John Rolfe

A SPORTS ILLUSTRATED FOR KIDS BOOK

First Edition

Library of Congress Cataloging-in-Publication Data

Rolfe, John
   David Robinson / John Rolfe. — 1st ed.
      p.   cm.
   "A Sports illustrated for kids book."
   Summary: Examines the life of the first graduate of the United States Naval Academy to play in the National Basketball Association.
   ISBN 0-316-75461-7
   1. Robinson, David, 1965——Juvenile literature. 2. Basketball players — United States — Biography — Juvenile Literature.
   [1. Robinson, David, 1965-. 2. Basketball players. 3. Afro-Americans — Biography.] I. Title.
   GV884.R615R65 1991
   796.323'092 — dc20   90-55742

SPORTS ILLUSTRATED FOR KIDS is a trademark of THE TIME INC. MAGAZINE COMPANY

Sports Illustrated For Kids Books is an imprint of Little, Brown and Company.

10 9 8 7 6 5 4 3 2 1

SEM

For further information regarding this title, write to Little, Brown and Company, 34 Beacon Street, Boston, MA 02108

Published simultaneously in Canada by Little, Brown & Company (Canada) Limited

Printed in the United States of America

Written by John Rolfe
Cover photograph by William B. Smith/Sports Illustrated
Cover design by Pegi Goodman
Comic strip illustrations by Brad Hamann
Interior line art by Jane Davila
Produced by Angel Entertainment, Inc.

Contents

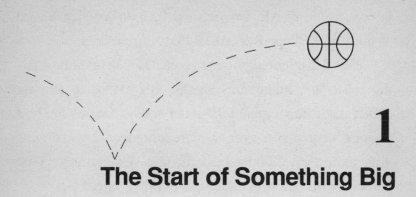

1

The Start of Something Big

The first game of a new season is an exciting and hopeful time. For some teams and their fans, it is a time to dream about winning a championship. For others, it is a time to forget about the losses of the past and make a new start.

For the fans and players of the San Antonio Spurs of the National Basketball Association (NBA), the first game of the 1989-90 season was particularly special. That night, a handsome, 7'1" center named David Robinson played his first regular season game for the Spurs.

David had been one of the greatest college basketball players of all time. During his four years at the United States Naval Academy, he set 33 school records and won many honors, including All-America and the John Wooden Award as the 1987 College Basketball Player of the Year.

David had scored points in bunches with his soft shooting touch and thunderous dunks. His explosive leaping ability made him a great rebounder and he became the first major college player ever to score more than 2,500 points, grab more than 1,300 rebounds, and sink more than 60 percent of his field-goal attempts during a career.

David was also exceptionally quick for a big man who weighed 235 pounds. His quickness made him a formidable defensive player and he set a major college career record by blocking 516 shots.

People expected David to join Hakeem Olajuwon [*o-LYE-je-won*]of the Houston Rockets and Patrick Ewing of the New York Knicks as one of the NBA's best centers. Some believed that he could be as good as all-time greats Wilt Chamberlain, who played mainly for the Philadelphia 76ers in the 1960's and the L.A. Lakers in the early 1970's. David expected great things of himself too.

"I want to be one of the top four centers in the league," he said. "That's what I should be, at least."

It was only natural that the Spurs' fans would be excited

that a player as good as David was joining their team. But there was another reason why his first game was so special: David, the Spurs, and the people of San Antonio, Texas, had been waiting two years for it.

Most NBA players join their teams right after they leave college. David had been required to serve two years in the Navy after he graduated from the Naval Academy in May 1987. The Spurs still thought he was worth waiting for. He was the first player chosen in the NBA draft that year.

During his two years in the Navy, David had been stationed at the Kings Bay submarine base in Georgia where he supervised construction projects. He was allowed to play for the United States basketball team at the 1987 Pan American Games and the 1988 Summer Olympics. But the time had passed slowly and he had grown eager to play regularly.

"The two years have seemed like ten," he said after he arrived at the Spurs' training camp in October 1989. "The people of San Antonio have had to be patient and I've had to be patient. I feel the anticipation as the season nears. I haven't felt this way in a long time. This is a new challenge and I love challenges."

One of the biggest challenges he faced was saving the

Spurs, who had not had a winning season since 1983. The year before David arrived, the team's 21-61 record was the worst in its 22-year history. Attendance at home games had been so low that the Spurs were in danger of being moved to another city. San Antonio needed a big star to attract fans and the team paid David $26 million to play for eight years.

"If David had not come here, this franchise was in the pits," said Red McCombs, the Spurs' owner. "David being here is so much more important to San Antonio than it would be to any other city in the NBA because this is the only professional sports team this city has. It will be exciting for us. But I think David's arrival is exciting to the entire basketball world."

David wasn't a beginner when it came to attracting fans and turning a weak team into a strong one. He had made the Navy basketball team a national attraction in 1987 when he led the Midshipmen to their first appearance in the national college basketball championship tournament in 25 years. The next year he led them to within one game of "The Final Four," the tournament's semifinals.

Even though David had been so successful in college, there was one big question being asked about him: Was he still able to play basketball as well as he had for Navy?

The answer wasn't clear. No one from the Naval Academy had ever played in the NBA before. Only a few Navy athletes, such as Roger Staubach, a quarterback for the Dallas Cowboys from 1969 to 1979, had played pro sports. Athletes who attend the Academy must serve in the Navy for up to five years after graduation. When they get out of the service, they are often 26 or 27 years old, which is usually too old to begin playing as a pro.

David was only 23 when he got out of the Navy, but during his two years at Kings Bay he had been unable to practice and play regularly. His skills became rusty and he played poorly for the U.S. team in the Pan Am Games and the Olympics. When Team USA failed to win gold medals at those tournaments, David was blamed.

"For a while, I blamed myself," he says. "I was a big part of both of those teams, we were expected to win and we didn't. I was the team leader. I felt really bad. I got down on myself and felt like maybe I didn't have that special magic."

Many other people also wondered. "He hasn't demonstrated up to now that he's got what the great ones had," said Jack McCloskey, the general manager of the Detroit Pistons.

Larry Brown, the Spurs' head coach, disagreed. During summer scrimmages and in training camp, David had shown flashes of his old talent. Coach Brown was confident that his new star would shine in the NBA. "There's no doubt in my mind he's going to be great, but it's going to take him time," he said. "The expectations are so high, I don't know if he'll ever satisfy everybody. But he satisfies me."

As for David, he was on a mission. "This season has extra special meaning for me," he said. "It's kind of a little deal with me, to prove myself, that I can make a difference. It's going to be a tremendous challenge: being away for two years and coming back against the best guys I've ever played against. But I'll get it done. I'm the type of person who if somebody says I can't do something, I'll guarantee you I'll get it done."

True to his word, David got it done in his very first game. The Spurs' opponents that night were the mighty Los Angeles Lakers, who had reached the NBA Championship finals the year before. The talented Lakers were led by their great guard, Magic Johnson, and their star forward, James Worthy. A crowd of 15,868 fans filled the HemisFair Arena in San Antonio to see how David would do against them.

David was nervous before the game. His stomach was so upset that he was able to play only 16 minutes during the first half. It didn't seem to matter, though. The Lakers had a hard time stopping David. They quickly fouled him three times as he drove for baskets. Meanwhile, his teammates gave the Lakers all they could handle. When the Spurs entered the locker room at halftime, they led 48-47.

By the time play resumed, David felt better and he began to show the crowd what they had come to see. In the third quarter, the Spurs were leading 72-70 when Magic Johnson went up for a layup. David batted it away and the Spurs were off and running. They scored the next three baskets, took control of the game, and out-hustled the Lakers to win 106-98. David led San Antonio with 23 points and 17 rebounds. It was an impressive debut.

"David is just learning, but I know he's going to be a great one," said Spurs forward Terry Cummings. "I haven't seen a guy that big who moves like he does. He definitely is going to be great."

Magic Johnson added, "Some rookies are never really rookies. Robinson's one of them."

Just as the people of San Antonio had hoped, opening

night was the beginning of a special season. David went on to lead the Spurs to a 56-26 record and a first-place finish in the Midwest Division. The team's 35-win improvement over the year before set an NBA record. David made the NBA All-Star team and finished second in the league in rebounds with 12.0 per game, third in blocked shots with 3.89 per game, and tied for ninth in scoring with a 24.3 points per game average.

David's performance earned him the NBA's Rookie of the Year Award and a place among the league's biggest stars. He also showed that there may be almost no limit to how good he can be.

"He's the most amazing athlete," Coach Brown said. "He has good instincts for basketball as well as his athletic ability. If he decides he wants to be the best and spends the time and works on it like Hakeem Olajuwon and Pat Ewing and some of the other guys, he has a chance to be the best."

Surprisingly, David didn't begin playing basketball seriously until his senior year in high school. That's pretty amazing if you think about how good he has become. Most NBA players have been playing the sport almost from the time they were able to walk.

"He's not your typical basketball junkie who played all the time," Coach Brown says. "It's amazing. He didn't start playing until recently and I think every day is a learning process for him. But he's bright and he wants to do well."

Learning has always been David's passion. That's why he chose to attend the Naval Academy. He wanted to be an engineer and his father, who had served in the Navy for 20 years, told him the Academy was a good place to get the education and training he needed.

David joined Navy's basketball team as a freshman, but the game was only a pleasant pastime for him. "Basketball was okay," he says. "It was something else to do. It was something challenging for me to try and learn."

David didn't become a star until his sophomore year, but he decided to stay at the Academy rather than transfer to another school where he would be able to join an NBA team immediately after graduation. At the time, David wasn't sure how much he liked basketball. He didn't find out until his junior and senior years when he blossomed into one of the biggest college basketball stars in the country. Even then, he did not realize that he would eventually become one of the best centers in the NBA.

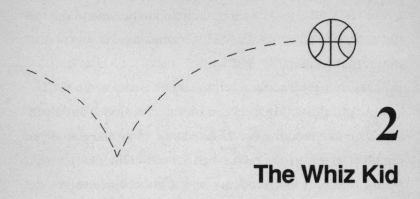

2
The Whiz Kid

David Maurice Robinson was born on August 6, 1965, in Key West, Florida. His family later moved to Virginia and David grew up near the city of Norfolk, where a major naval base is located. He was the second of three children. His sister, Kimberly, is two years older and his brother, Chuck, is six years younger.

It was only natural that David would one day join the Navy. His father, Ambrose, and his grandfather, who was also named Ambrose, were both Navy men, although they did not attend the Academy as David and Chuck later did.

At the time David was born, his mother, Freda, was working as a nurse while his dad was a Chief Petty Officer serving in the Navy as a sonar technician. Sonar is a device that is used to detect underwater objects by bouncing sound waves off of them.

David's father is an intelligent and dedicated man. He had grown up in Little Rock, Arkansas, at a time when black people in the South were not allowed to attend the same schools or eat in the same restaurants as white people. Because of these and other reasons, blacks had to work twice as hard as whites to succeed. Life had not been easy for Mr. Robinson, but he learned to be very determined in everything he did. His experience in the Navy also taught him to be disciplined and patient.

Ambrose and Freda Robinson wanted David, Chuck, and Kimberly to be confident but not cocky. They did not want their children to set limits. "My parents told me that anything in life is attainable if you want it badly enough," David says. "I've gotten almost all my ideas from them."

David was a very bright and curious child. "Anything and everything that went on, he wanted to know what and why," his dad says. "David wanted to know it all."

Mr. Robinson was interested in electronics, carpentry, and music. David was always asking him questions about what he was doing, so his dad taught him how to take apart and rebuild TV sets and how to make his own electronic gadgets. He showed David how to play simple chords on the piano, which David later used to teach himself how to play.

David was also fascinated by books. He liked to stay up late at night reading science fiction. His favorite stories were *The Magic of Xanth*, which is a collection of novels by Piers Anthony. "I used to wonder how much of it was true," David says.

When David was in first grade, his parents entered him in classes for gifted children. He was especially talented in math. He often amazed his mom by adding up the cost of the groceries she was putting in her shopping cart when they were at the supermarket. By the time his mom got to the checkout counter, David already knew exactly how much she would have to pay. He had done the addition in his head!

David liked to put his mind to making money, too. He had a paper route and he mowed lawns. "He would do anything for a little money," says his mom. "He was a little hustler, and I do not mean that negatively. What I mean is that he was always a hard worker."

Working hard and keeping busy with new interests kept

David out of trouble as he was growing up. Well, almost. "When I was little, I used to hang out with another little kid and we'd pick up cigar butts and smoke them," he says. "But I guess I never did anything really bad."

David was a very friendly and outgoing kid with lots of friends. The other kids in his neighborhood gave him the nickname "Godfrey" after the actor, Godfrey Cambridge, whom David resembled whenever he talked excitedly.

David liked sports. He played pickup games of all kinds with friends and was good in just about every sport he tried. He played baseball, football, and tennis. He won a peewee golf tournament when he was 12. When his dad bought a pool table, David quickly learned the game. He began beating his dad so often that Mr. Robinson got frustrated and sold the table! David liked tumbling and gymnastics. During family trips to the beach, he would do somersaults on the sand dunes. "I've always been a flipping fanatic," he says.

Oddly, David wasn't very turned on by basketball. He watched NBA games on TV and he liked the Philadelphia 76ers, but playing the game did not really excite him. Sometimes he would go to the playground with his friends and while they shot baskets, he would do gymnastics.

David did not play organized basketball until he was in eighth grade. He was a forward on his school's team, but he didn't start or even play very much. He worried that practice and games were interfering with his schoolwork, so he quit the team after the season.

At that time, David was more interested in electronics than dunks and dribbles. He began taking computer courses at a local college and surprised his family by building a six-foot TV projection screen for them.

The screen had been bought by David's dad for $1,800 as a kit, the way model cars and airplanes are sold. His dad planned to put it together, but the Navy sent him out to sea on a ship for three weeks. While his dad was gone, David took out the kit and built the screen. Mr. Robinson was amazed to find it standing in the family's den when he returned home. "Then David went down to the store and helped them fix their display model," he says.

By the time David entered 10th grade, he was dreaming of becoming an engineer. His dad told him that the Naval Academy would be a good college for him to get his engineering degree. The Academy trains men and women to be Naval officers. They learn how to repair and operate the

Navy's ships and planes and how naval bases are run. After graduation, they must serve in the Navy for up to five years.

To get into the Naval Academy, a person must have good grades as well as a recommendation from a senator or congressman. David knew that he would have to work very hard so that he would be accepted when he applied for admission to the school. His work and effort paid off. When David took his college entrance exams, which are called SAT's (Standard Aptitude Tests), as a junior in high school, his score was 1,320 points out of a possible 1,600!

At the end of David's junior year, his dad retired from the Navy and got a job in Washington, D.C., where he worked for a company that made military equipment. The Robinsons then moved to Manassas, Virginia, and David transferred to Osbourn Park High.

The new kid in school quickly caught the eye of the other students. David had grown 10 inches in four years and was 6'7" tall. "The minute he was here, every kid in the halls was on him to play basketball," says Art Payne, who was the coach of Osbourn Park's varsity team. "You couldn't miss his size."

David hadn't been thinking about basketball very

15

much. He wasn't too interested in joining the team until Coach Payne spotted him walking in the hall one day and asked him if he wanted to try out.

"We had started practice, but we hadn't played any games yet," Coach Payne says. "He came in the next day. We had a center, a six-foot, six-inch kid, but he got hurt and David took his place."

David scored 14 points and grabbed 14 rebounds in his first game. It was clear he had talent, but Coach Payne could tell David hadn't played much. "In the short time he played for me, I never had a player with the touch he had with the ball and he had great hands," he says. "The only thing he lacked was experience. He didn't have any experience of high school coaching and playing, but he picked things up really fast. I didn't know his potential would develop."

David didn't know that it would either. "I don't know what my potential was in high school," he says. "Basketball was something extra to do, but that was it. It was no big deal. I never thought about it going anywhere. For a while, I never even thought about playing in college."

David found that he hated practice and his mind often wandered during games. He also had a hard time getting used to his coach's yelling. One day when the team played poorly, Coach Payne chewed his squad out during halftime. As he yelled, he stood right in front of David, who sat staring straight ahead. He was stunned by Coach Payne's outburst.

David played pretty well that season. He averaged about 15 points and 12 rebounds per game. Those numbers aren't spectacular, but they were good enough to earn him the team's MVP award, all-district and all-area honors.

David also attracted the interest of basketball recruiters from such colleges as Harvard, Holy Cross, George Mason University, and the Naval Academy. David was surprised that anyone was interested in him as a player.

During the season, Paul Evans, the coach of Navy's basketball team, received a phone call from a Naval officer who lived in David's hometown. The officer told Coach Evans there was a big kid playing for Osbourn Park High whom he should go see. Coach Evans decided to take a look.

"David was a skinny kid who could run, but he couldn't do much else," Coach Evans recalls. "His team got beat by 25 points that night. Actually, there were two kids I was looking at. At first glance, I was more impressed with the other one."

Coach Evans kept an eye on David for the rest of the year. He could see that David was improving. His shooting skills were getting better each game. Coach Evans decided that David might develop into a pretty decent player. He also knew that David was interested in attending the Academy.

"David was sincerely interested in an education," he says. "His father had given him some insight into a Naval career and I think the idea of becoming a Naval officer appealed to him. The education certainly did."

Coach Evans was very impressed by David's wide variety of interests, especially after he visited the Robinsons' house and saw the TV screen David had built. "As a student, he was very good," he recalls. "He got his share of A's. With his score on the college entrance exams, we knew he wouldn't have a problem at the Academy."

David talked to a couple of schools and then decided to go to the Academy. "I needed a challenge," he says. "I was pretty lazy in high school and never had to work for anything. Good grades came easy, everything came easy."

To be sure, David would be challenged at the Naval Academy. Nothing came easy there.

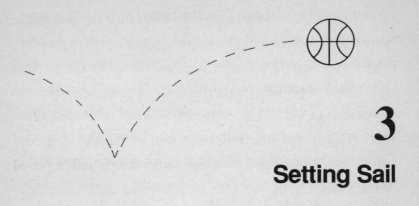

3

Setting Sail

David's unlikely voyage to basketball stardom began on a hot July day in 1983 when he arrived at the United States Naval Academy in Annapolis, Maryland.

Dressed in a pair of jeans and a casual shirt, David spent the day with his new classmates filling out forms and receiving uniforms and dormitory assignments. "We were standing in all these different lines waiting to go to all these different places," he says. "I remember it being a long day."

At the end of the long afternoon, the new midshipmen were sworn in. "Then they started yelling at us and telling us where to go," David remembers. "Most of the day, they were pretty polite. Then they weren't polite at all. I remember thinking, 'What have I gotten myself into?' I didn't get much sleep that first night. I didn't know what to expect those first few weeks."

David shared a room with Carl "Hootie" Liebert in Bancroft Hall where 137 midshipmen lived. There were no TVs in the dorm and only one telephone. David made himself feel more at home by setting up a stereo system he had rigged.

Life at the Academy was demanding. David and the other midshipmen had to get up early each morning and report for marching drills at 7:30 AM. Then they attended four hours of classes, ate lunch, and went back to classes until late afternoon. In the evening, there were more marching drills, then study hours and bedtime.

With so much to do each day, keeping up with schoolwork was difficult. "Homework? It varied from too much to way too much," David says. "At first, everything seemed unfair. No radio, no TV in the hall, no McDonald's. But what you get at the end, the responsibility, the respect, the security, keeps you going. You learn to cope, not complain, and problems don't bother you after a while."

Hootie Liebert could see that his roommate liked the

Naval Academy. "David loved the security of the place," he says. "The idea of someone telling him when to eat, sleep, work, play. The only negative was [loss of] freedom and David wasn't a drinker or partier, so he didn't need that."

Even with a busy daily schedule, there was still time at the Academy for sports. The midshipmen were required to take gym classes that included boxing, gymnastics, swimming, and diving. Some of the classes were very tough. In swimming class, for example, midshipmen were made to swim continuously for 40 minutes. They were also told to dive off a tower that was almost 33 feet high. It took David a while to conquer his fear, but he learned to make the dive eventually without thinking.

David stood out among his classmates because he was so tall, but attracting attention was something David did not really want to do. "From Day One at the Academy, my first squad leader said to be inconspicuous," he says. "He figured that as tall as I was, I'd stand out like a big, sore thumb. And at the Academy, everybody just wants to blend in. Nobody wants to be known."

The other midshipmen quickly noticed how graceful and athletic David was. "We were required to take a three-week course in gymnastics," Hootie Liebert recalls. "Dave was so big, I didn't think he could do it. We'd looked bad and then Dave gets on the parallel bars and starts doing all sorts of stuff. It took him one week to do all the required stuff and get an A."

David tried out for the basketball team, but he did not take the game seriously. "I figured basketball would just be an outlet, something else I could do so I wouldn't get all wrapped up in school," he says. "At the Academy, it's nice to have as many distractions as you can."

Basketball proved to be more of a distraction than David had expected. In his first practice scrimmages, he had to play against 6'7" forward Vernon Butler, who was the team's best player. Butler was called "Captain Crunch" for his physical style of play, and sometimes Coach Evans made David and Vernon battle each other in rebounding drills.

"I got beat up every day," David says. "I caught a lot of elbows. I spent a lot of time protecting my nose. I was getting my face beat up. The game didn't come naturally to me and basketball was more work than fun. I knew I would prove myself academically, so I wanted to stick it out. I just wanted to play so I could get my varsity letter."

David found that playing basketball made it difficult to keep his grades up. Having to practice each day cut into his study time. "The daily schedule is so regimented," he says. "The same thing every day and it keeps you really busy. When you come back from practice, you're tired. Get up in the morning and you're tired from something you did yesterday."

David spent his free time sleeping, chatting with other midshipmen, or dropping by the dorm's lounge to play a song or two on the piano. He was amazed that his roommate, who was also on the basketball team, preferred to practice instead. "He couldn't understand why I'd be out shooting baskets late at night," Hootie Liebert says. "He used to ask me, 'Don't you get tired of working out and playing?'"

David did not play much his first season. He missed the team's first four games after he broke his hand in boxing class, but it didn't matter. He was not a starter anyway. He played only about 13 minutes per game and scored an average of 7.6 points.

Coach Evans saw that David had the potential to be a good player by the way he ran up and down the court, but he didn't like the fact that David was often lazy in practice.

Yet he decided not to yell at David too often because he didn't want him to quit. "I can be the biggest jerk in the world to try and push a kid if I think it's the right thing to do," he says. "But I think if I had done that with David, he might just have walked away."

The other players on the team saw David's potential, too. They also liked having him around because he was a friendly person to hang out with. They nicknamed him "Country," as in "Country Bumpkin," after they learned that he had never flown in an airplane and had never been inside a hotel or a bar.

David's freshman year was a quiet one, but he did make one thing clear — he had demonstrated the kind of athletic talent that would one day make him a star.

"He's so good at everything, it's disgusting," Hootie Liebert says. "I wish there was just one sport I could beat him at. The guy can shoot a great round of golf, play tennis well. I thought I could get him at squash because he's so big inside that little court. But no, he beat me at that, too."

David did not know when he went home in the spring of 1984 that basketball would soon be the sport that would make him famous.

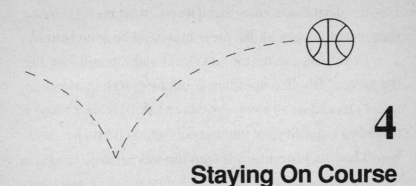

4

Staying On Course

David spent the summer playing basketball in the Urban Coalition League in Washington, D.C. He had not yet fallen in love with the game, but he wanted to improve his skills just to see how good he could become. He also ran and lifted weights to get in shape for his sophomore season.

By the time David returned to Annapolis in the fall, he had developed an excellent shooting touch. He was quicker and more agile, and he had grown three inches. He was now 6'11" and the tallest player in Navy history.

Coach Evans was pleased when he saw how much David had improved. Navy had had a fine season the year before, finishing with a 24-8 record without much help from

David. Coach Evans knew that if he could get David to make the most of his new skills, the team would be even better.

Coach Evans liked the fact that David was still learning the game. "It's like coaching a ninth-or 10th-grader," he said. "David doesn't have a lot of bad habits. It's a lot easier to teach a kid with great intelligence, which David has, if he hasn't had six years of learning it the other way."

David needed to work on his defensive skills and there were times when he wasn't sure where he should go on the court during certain plays. How well he would play that season depended on how hard he was willing to practice.

Finding time to work on basketball was tough once again. David's courses that year included such demanding subjects as physics, computer science, advanced calculus, and thermodynamics, which is the study of how moving objects produce heat.

It didn't take long for David to learn that he could produce an awesome amount of heat on the basketball court. In Navy's third game that season, David scorched American University for 29 points and 11 rebounds in an impressive 84-68 win. His performance drew raves from Ed Tapscott, American's head coach. "Robinson's one of the top big men

26

in the east, no doubt about it," he said. "He's definitely got pro potential."

Four days later, David caught fire in the Saluki Shootout Tournament. In Navy's first game against Southern Illinois, he scored 31 points. The next night, against Western Illinois, he scored 37 to become the first Navy player in 18 years to score 30 or more points two games in a row. In four games that week, including two at the tournament, David scored a total of 115 points, grabbed 52 rebounds, and won the Saluki Shootout MVP award.

David was stunned by what he had done. "It was pretty incredible," he says. "It was the first time I got an idea of what I could do."

Hootie Liebert said that after the game against Western Illinois, David turned to him and said, "Wow, I can play!"

The rest of the country thought so too. Newspapers and magazines ran stories about Navy's amazing center. David was surprised to learn that he had become a big-time player. "I never thought of myself as a big-time basketball player," he said. "I still don't, really. In high school, basketball was just something I sort of experimented with. It was never a big thing to me. Now I work hard at it because I think I have the potential to be good. But if I don't become a big star, it isn't that big a deal to me. I still play for fun."

After the Saluki Shootout, the Navy basketball team was given a four-week break so the players could take exams. David dove back into his schoolwork, but he soon heard talk in the media that he might leave Navy after the school year ended. Many stories about him said that he was good enough to play pro basketball. If he transferred to another college, he would not have to serve in the Navy after graduation. He could join an NBA team right away.

The idea of playing pro basketball was beyond David's wildest dreams. "When people bring up pro basketball to me, I laugh," he said. "I don't think of myself that way. Basketball is just one thing I do. When people ask me about transferring, I say, 'I haven't thought about it' because if no one asked me, I never would have thought about it at all."

Coach Evans wasn't concerned about the rumors that this might be David's last year at the Academy. "David loves going to school here," he told reporters. "He's a great student, and he really wants to get his degree here. I'm not saying it's impossible, but I think he'll stay."

Almost every day, David was reminded that he could

make a lot of money as a pro player. The idea tempted him, and he even admitted that he was thinking about it during an interview on national television. "You can't help but have it on your mind," he said. "Playing basketball for $200,000, $300,000 a year, that sounds like the best life of all."

The more David thought about leaving the Academy, the more he wondered how good a player he really was. "Maybe I don't think I'm as good as other people seem to think I am," he said. "Right now, I don't see any reason to leave Navy. It's a tough place, but I'm happy here. I enjoy the academics. We spend the right amount of time on basketball here. I spend as much time in the dorm as I do playing ball."

David's father told reporters that the decision was entirely up to his son. "I hope he stays," he added. "He's so at home there he forgets to call home here."

When the season resumed in early January, David looked more at home on the court than ever. He led the Midshipmen to 10 wins in a row. By the end of the month, he was among the Division I college leaders in scoring average (22.9 points per game), rebounding (10.5 per game), and field goal percentage (.650).

With David leading the way, the Midshipmen attracted attention as they never had before and their home games in Halsey Field House were jammed. "I have been a Navy basketball watcher since the mid-1930's," said Al Hopkins, the sports editor of *The Annapolis Capital*. "There has never been so much interest and excitement in a Navy team. There were days not too long ago when you could count the midshipmen and town people at the game on your fingers."

But even though David had become a star player, there were still times when he was lazy. Coach Evans had to bawl him out every now and then. In a game against Lafayette, David missed five free throws in a row during the first half and did not play aggressively. Coach Evans pulled him out of the game and made him sit on the bench for a while. That woke David up. In the second half, he went on a scoring tear and finished with 27 points as Navy won 74-71.

The Midshipmen finished the regular season with an outstanding 22-5 record. They won the next three games in a row to take the East Coast Athletic Conference (ECAC) South Tournament and became the first Navy team since 1960 to qualify for the National Collegiate Athletic Association (NCAA) Championship Tournament.

It was an impressive achievement. Even though Navy lost to Maryland in the second round, David and his teammates were cheered when they returned to Annapolis. They had put Navy in the national spotlight, and served notice that they had become one of the best teams in college basketball.

David finished the season with 756 points. That total broke a school record that had stood for 31 years. He had also set Navy records by scoring 30 points or more in a game eight times and by sinking 302 field goals. His rebounding average of 11.6 per game was the best by a Navy player in 30 years. He won all-conference honors and was chosen as the ECAC South Player of the Year.

Once again there was talk that David would leave Navy. He was contacted by officials from schools such as Notre Dame, UCLA, Kentucky, Georgetown, and Indiana. These schools had famous basketball programs. Suddenly, David was forced to make the most important decision of his life: Did he want to stay at Navy, earn his degree, and then serve as a Naval officer for five years, or did he want to transfer so he could concentrate on becoming a pro basketball player?

It was a tough choice. If David stayed at the Academy, he would be guaranteed a job in the Navy that would pay him $20,000 a year plus his food, housing, and travel costs. After five years he could try to become a pro basketball player, but he would be 27 years old by then. David knew that a Navy athlete had never played in the NBA before. However, if he left the Academy, he would not be allowed to play basketball at his new school for one year, although he could still keep his skills sharp for his senior season. Then he could hope to be drafted by an NBA team that could pay him hundreds of thousands, if not millions, of dollars.

"I had to make a decision," he says. "We are talking about a lot of money. I don't live for money. I mean, it is important to me. But a lot of people think you are automatically happy if you have a lot of money. I don't necessarily believe that is true."

David told reporters that he would announce his decision during the first week in April. Then he spent a lot of time thinking. He laid on his bed at night and stared at the ceiling while he wondered what to do. He talked with his parents, coach, and friends, as well as Academy officials.

The officials told David that if he stayed at the Acad-

32

emy, he might not have to serve a full five-year commitment in the Navy. They couldn't promise that they would shorten his service commitment, but they told him not to stop thinking about playing pro basketball either.

Coach Evans began to suspect that David was going to stay at the Academy after David told him, "I like basketball, and it's a challenge, but it is one of a number of parts of my life. If I have to, I can live without it. No question about it."

While the world of basketball waited for David's decision, Coach Evans told reporters, "Robinson is smart enough that he is not letting the media bother him. The media talks about him transferring. He doesn't. He probably could make as much money as an engineer as he could as a basketball player."

Finally, David announced that he was going to stay at the Academy. A Navy spokesman read a statement from David to reporters: "The Academy has been good for me and I want the chance to receive a degree from here. Pro ball? I guess I still have a hard time visualizing myself playing at that level with all those great players. I want to improve on what we accomplished this year. Everyone is saying I'm great, but who can you listen to? I'm in control. I'm doing what I want to do. I have no regrets. I came here for academics, but all my goals got cloudy. The press confused me a lot. Basketball came so fast. It really just came together this year. I'm still in my early stages. I don't know how much basketball means to me right now."

David's decision to stay at the Naval Academy made him a national hero. He was applauded by sportswriters and political leaders who said David was a wonderful example for young people. "David Robinson chose to stay at Navy," said Mario Cuomo, the governor of New York, during a speech on national radio. "He talked about commitment, loyalty, and values. I wonder how many of us would choose these virtues rather than the chance of becoming a millionaire, especially if you were a college sophomore when you had to make that choice."

David made the choice he did because he had listened to his heart. "My experience with the Navy had been good, so I went with the flow," he says. "Fulfilling my commitment was the right thing to do."

As the future would show, it was the right thing to do. But there would be times during the next few years when David would wonder if he had made a mistake.

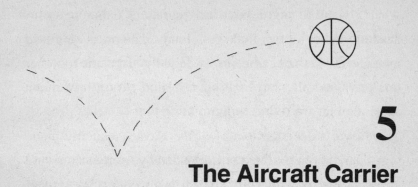

5

The Aircraft Carrier

Before the start of David's junior year, Coach Evans was walking through the parking lot of a restaurant near the Academy one day. Suddenly, a voice called out, "Hey, Coach! Look what I learned last summer!" Coach Evans turned around and there was David walking on his hands across the parking lot!

That summer, David had learned more than just how to walk on his hands. He had been chosen to play for a team of college all-stars that had played in the Jones Cup Tournament in Europe. David's teammates were some of the best young players in the country and they had impressed him with their hard work and dedication to basketball.

"It was 105 degrees during practice and these guys were busting it every day," he says. "They never wanted to stop playing. It was kind of inspiring. I had to keep my mind in the game and play hard myself or I'd get absolutely killed. Even though we didn't win anything that summer, I really gained a lot of confidence."

David brought that confidence and determination back to the Academy and it proved to be the key to his best season yet. His teammates noticed the change in him right away.

"This year he is talking about how he can't wait to practice," Hootie Liebert told reporters. "I have never heard him say that before."

Vernon Butler said, "Last year, David was hesitant sometimes. No more. This year he has confidence and you can see it in his eyes when he decides to go to the hoop. When he wants to go, he's going."

Great things were expected of David and his teammates in the coming season. A pre-season poll of basketball writers had ranked Navy among the top 20 teams in the country, and many people were calling David the best center in the college game.

"I think the best center we played against last year was

that kid from Navy, Dave Robinson," remarked Lefty Driesell, the head coach of the Maryland team that had beaten Navy in the 1985 NCAA Tournament. "If he keeps improving like that, he could be Patrick Ewing. The guy really impressed me."

Coach Evans agreed with Driesell. "With a little more work, David could be the best center in the country," he said.

David was determined to be the best. In a way, his new dedication to basketball was surprising because his chances of playing in the NBA were slim now that he had chosen to stay at the Academy. It would have been understandable if basketball had meant less to David than it had before. Some of his teammates on the college all-star team had told him he had made a mistake by not transferring to another college.

"Everyone told me I should have transferred, but I figured they would say that," he says. "I figured they would think I was crazy to say that money does not mean that much as long as I'm happy with what I'm doing and living comfortably. Hey, I have security. I have the Navy behind me. I have a place to work."

David's teammates at Navy hadn't expected him to feel that way. They knew what he had given up in order to stay at the Academy and they figured he would have second thoughts. Red Romo, the team's trainer, was convinced that David was having regrets when he saw David sulking at practice one day. As it turned out, David was upset because he had failed a math test.

The Midshipmen got off to a flying start that season by winning seven of their first 10 games. David played spectacularly, averaging 21.2 points, 13.7 rebounds, and 3.4 blocked shots per game in those 10 games. He also won all-tournament honors at the Carrier Classic, the Suntory Ball, and the Cotton State Classic.

In Navy's 11th game, David scored 21 points, grabbed 14 rebounds, and set a Navy record by blocking 14 shots in a 76-61 win over North Carolina-Wilmington. He kept rolling by totaling 68 points, 43 rebounds, and 25 blocks in Navy's next three games. All three were victories and *Sports Illustrated* named David the magazine's player of the week.

With all the recognition David received, he could have become lazy or conceited. But he actually grew more determined. "The more recognition he's gotten," Coach Evans told reporters, "the harder he's worked at basketball."

There was a negative side to all the attention — it

constantly reminded David about what he had given up by choosing to stay at the Academy. Yet he stuck to his guns. "I stand by my decision," he said. "I do think about it sometimes. Rafael Addison [a player at Syracuse University] is a good friend of mine. Just talking to him about going to the pros and then reading, 'Robinson did this or that, but he can't play pros,' sometimes it's tough."

David couldn't spend too much time thinking about it, though, because he had plenty of schoolwork to keep him busy. His courses that year included electrical engineering, history of science and technology, American literature, and advanced computer programming. Finding time to study was difficult. One night David returned to his dorm room after a game against Delaware in which he had scored 37 points and grabbed 14 rebounds. He was exhausted, but he stayed up late working on a computer program he had been assigned to write. Then he got up extra-early the next morning to finish the assignment.

Navy officials acknowledged that David was too tall to serve on ships or planes after he graduated. He would most likely be stationed at a Naval base for five years instead.

The announcement did not surprise David. After he

returned from Europe the summer before, he had spent a week aboard a submarine, the U.S.S. Buffalo. The ceilings in the submarine were only six feet high and the living quarters were so tiny that David had to hunch over all the time and duck through doorways. He had also scrunched himself into the cockpit of a fighter plane in Pensacola, Florida, for a training flight. He knew from those uncomfortable experiences that he was indeed too big to serve on ships or planes.

It was now possible that David could play for an NBA team if the team played its home games in a city near the base where he was stationed. Reporters asked David if he was interested in playing pro ball even if he could only play in his team's home games. "If there was a way, I definitely would think about it," he replied. "But I'm under the impression there is no way."

David was right, but he did not realize at the time that the stage was being set for him to serve only two years in the Navy instead of the required five. In the meantime, he continued his rampage on the basketball court.

February was an incredible month. The Midshipmen won nine games in a row. They began the streak by beating

North Carolina-Wilmington 95-68. David scored 31 points and caused Mel Gibson, North Carolina-Wilmington's head coach, to remark that "the only way to stop Robinson is with long chains and handcuffs."

On February 12, David grabbed 25 rebounds in a 78-53 win over Fairfield at the Meadowlands Arena, the home of the NBA's New Jersey Nets. No player, college or pro, had ever had so many rebounds in one game at that arena.

As David continued to reach new heights, sportscasters began comparing him to the all-time greats. "He's a Bill Russell who can score," remarked Doug Collins, a basketball broadcaster for CBS-TV. Al McGuire, another basketball broadcaster, nicknamed David "The Aircraft Carrier" for the way he carried Navy to victory night after night.

While Navy rolled along, David convinced many NBA officials that he was good enough to play professionally even if he did have to wait five years to do it.

"He's a pro prospect, one of the better big men in college," said Pat Williams, the general manager of the Philadelphia 76ers. "Down the road, after his service obligation, he can be an NBA player. He won't be an old man at 27."

The way David saw it, he couldn't lose no matter what happened. "I'll probably go to supply school," he said. "It will be good business background if the NBA doesn't work out, or afterward if it does."

David and the Midshipmen couldn't lose on the court, either. They finished the regular season with a 10-game winning streak that gave them a 24-4 record and their second conference championship in a row. Then they swept through the conference tournament with three more wins. In the first one, against James Madison, David scored 32 points to set a Navy record. It was the 13th time in his college career that he had scored 30 points or more in a game. In the third game, David scored 26 points, grabbed 12 rebounds, and blocked six shots in a 72-61 win over George Mason.

David's hot performance earned him tournament MVP honors, and the win over George Mason earned the Midshipmen another appearance in the NCAA tournament. David was also chosen as the conference's player of the year.

To be sure, it had been a special season. David looked back over the road he had traveled to stardom and praised the other Midshipmen for the help they had given him. "My teammates open the doors for me," he said. "When I first came here, I can remember how I got burned all the time. That was a rough time, something I changed with only a lot of hard work. Gradually, I've gained more confidence, but I know I've still got a long way to go."

As great as David had been, some people still pointed out that he had been playing against some of the weaker teams in college basketball. They also said that David wasn't always aggressive and that he lacked experience. For those reasons, they doubted that he would be able to help the Midshipmen get very far in the NCAA tournament.

But people underestimated the ability of the rest of the Navy team. Along with David and Vernon Butler, Navy had guards Kylor Whitaker and Doug Wojcik who could each score with accurate shots from farther back on the court.

Navy proved that they were for real in their first NCAA tournament game against a tough team from Tulsa University. David poured home 30 points, grabbed 12 rebounds, and blocked 5 shots. Vernon Butler scored 25 points and grabbed 11 rebounds. Navy won 87-68. When a reporter wondered after the game if Navy's win was a fluke, David replied, "I'd thought we'd already proved we weren't a fluke. I don't think we have to prove anything else."

But they did. Navy's next game was against the powerful Syracuse Orangemen, who had beaten the Midshipmen, 89-67, earlier that season. Navy's job looked even tougher because the game was going to be played on Syracuse's home court in the Carrier Dome.

At first, things did not look good for Navy. The crowd of 21,713 people in the Carrier Dome howled with delight as the Orangemen jumped out to a 17-8 lead. The Midshipmen had problems stopping Syracuse's fast break and had to call a timeout with 13:40 left in the first half.

The timeout gave the Midshipmen a chance to catch their breath and regroup. Then they began a patient comeback from a 21-14 deficit. Navy outscored Syracuse, 10-2, in the next few minutes. Then Vernon Butler muscled his way to the basket with 4:43 left in the half, giving the Midshipmen the lead for the first time, 24-23.

The lead seesawed back and forth until Navy's Derrick Turner made an acrobatic layup to give the Midshipmen a 32-31 edge as the halftime buzzer sounded. When the Navy players returned to their locker room, they weren't very pleased with themselves.

"We were mad," David says. "We had shot terribly or

we would have had a six or seven-point lead. We really wanted to get out and play in the second half."

With 17:10 left in the game, Syracuse took their last lead. It did not take long after that for the Midshipmen to take control of the game and silence the crowd. Vernon Butler scored to tie the game at 39-39; Navy would not trail again. Then David sank two free throws and dunked after Kylor Whitaker missed a shot. A few minutes later, some beautiful passing from Doug Wojcik to Cliff Rees to David led to a slam dunk that gave Navy a 55-46 lead.

The final 10 minutes of the game belonged to Navy. The Middies built their lead to 70-53 and iced a win that ended with a final score of 97-85. David fouled out of the game with almost three minutes left, but as he walked off the court, the crowd stood and applauded him.

David had bulldozed his way through the Orangemen for 35 points, 11 rebounds, and 7 blocked shots. He slammed home five dunks off alley-oop passes while holding Syracuse's center, Rony Seikaly, to only four points. David's teammates were just as hot. Vernon Butler scored 23 points and Doug Wojcik did a brilliant job of bringing the ball up the court whenever Navy went on the attack.

The Orangemen were stunned by what Navy had done. "I'm a little bit shocked," commented Pearl Washington, Syracuse's star forward. "We knew Navy had a good team but we didn't expect them to come in here and do this. The bottom line is, we had to stop David Robinson. He had 35 points. We had to stop Vernon Butler. He had 23 points. That says it all. They whipped us."

"David's as good a big man as there is in the country," said Jim Boeheim, Syracuse's head coach. "He took away our inside offense and we couldn't stop him at the other end. He just killed us."

David, however, wasn't impressed by his own performance that night. "I don't think I played that great," he told reporters after the game. "I did some good things defensively, but I didn't put it together."

As unimpressed as David was, the win over Syracuse made David the most talked-about player at the NCAA tournament. Sportswriters and broadcasters applauded him for his intelligence, his decision to stay in the Navy, and his commitment to academic excellence.

"Am I a role model to kids because I go to Navy and we don't have a bad reputation?" David asked reporters one day during the tournament. "Hey, you guys don't even know what I'm doing at Navy. It's exciting to be here, but my grades are really slipping. I've been spending too much time on basketball. But that's the most important thing. Right now, anyway."

David gave another impressive performance in Navy's next game. Cleveland State went crazy trying to stop him, but he ended up with 22 points, 14 rebounds, and 9 blocked shots. He also scored the winning basket with only six seconds left in the game. The final score was Navy 71, Cleveland State 70.

The Midshipmen were now only one win away from the Final Four, the tournament's semifinals. Their next opponent was the tough Duke University Blue Devils, who were favored to win the national championship. "I always look forward to these kinds of games," David said. "You get a chance to go out and show what you can do."

The anticipated Navy-Duke showdown was played at the Meadowlands Arena in New Jersey, on March 23, 1986. It was a tough battle from start to finish as Duke had three players guarding David at all times. He scored Navy's first seven points, but the Blue Devils kept overpowering the

Midshipmen in rebounding battles. Duke scored 20 of their first 32 points after grabbing rebounds of their own shots. Then just before the end of the first half, they outscored Navy, 18-2, to take a 34-22 lead.

Unfortunately for the Midshipmen, things did not improve in the second half. Guard Johnny Dawkins of Duke scored 14 points in the first 10 minutes and the Blue Devils began to put the game away. Their fans chanted "A-ban-don ship! A-ban-don ship!" as Navy tried as hard as they could to come back. David finished the game with 23 points and 10 rebounds, but it wasn't enough. Navy lost 71-50.

It was a disappointing end to a great season for David and the Midshipmen. Their final record was 30-5 and David received All-America honors. He was college basketball's leading rebounder with an average of 13 rebounds per game and its top shot-blocker with a 5.9 per game average. He was also ranked 14th in the country in scoring with a 22.7 points-per-game average and 16th in field-goal percentage (.607). No other college player had finished the season ranked among the country's top 20 in four statistical categories that year.

In spite of all of these wonderful achievements, David

was upset by the loss to Duke. He said that the Midshipmen had played like wimps and refused to talk to reporters for several weeks after the game. David's teammates weren't insulted by his remark. Instead, they saw it as a sign that David cared more about basketball than ever before.

"If David realizes he can be the best, he will be," remarked Pete Herrmann, the team's assistant coach. "I think he's ready. I think he really wants it now."

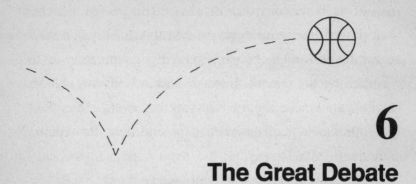

6

The Great Debate

The sting of Navy's loss to Duke in the NCAA tournament didn't last very long for David. Shortly after he left the Academy at the end of his junior year, David reported to Colorado Springs, Colorado, where tryouts for the U.S. National Basketball Team were held.

The team began preparing for the World Basketball Championships that would be held in Madrid, Spain, that summer. The world championships were an important event that the United States had won only once in nine appearances. The last time a U.S. team had won a gold medal there was in 1954. David and his teammates were determined to reverse that losing streak.

After David arrived in camp, the team's coaches noticed that the discipline of the Naval Academy had made an impression on the star center. "Every morning at six o'clock, when I was assigned to wake up all the players, Robinson was already up brushing his teeth," says Nick Bongopolous, a team assistant. "He said it was his routine at the Naval Academy."

The tryouts for the national team gave David the opportunity to test himself against the best college players in the country. Each day he scrimmaged against Kenny Smith, Tyrone "Muggsy" Bogues, Ronny Seikaly, Charles Smith, and several other players who are now playing in the NBA.

David showed that he had what it took to hold his own against such tough competition. Playing in a scrimmage, David led all scorers with 26 points, grabbed 12 rebounds, and blocked 5 shots in a 94-83 win. It was an impressive performance that was watched from the sidelines by basketball hall of famer Bill Russell.

Russell, a center who had led the Boston Celtics to 11 NBA championships between 1957 and 1969, had never seen David play before. "He's a very versatile player with a variety of skills," Russell said. "He's a good passer with good hand-eye coordination. He's got enormous potential."

David made the team easily. He then returned to the Navy and spent two weeks in Hawaii on an aircraft carrier. When that assignment ended, he traveled to Arizona, where the national team practiced twice a day for two weeks. Then the team left for France to play a series of exhibition games before the world championships began in late June.

It was a crazy trip. At the time, Europe had been hit by a wave of terrorist bombings. The targets were often American soldiers and bases, so it was feared that the U.S. team might be in danger, too.

When David and his teammates arrived in Madrid, Spain, there were soldiers on the roof of their hotel. "Everywhere we went, there were police cars and helicopters following the team bus," David said. "It made you feel a lot safer."

The basketball court was not a safe place to be if your opponent was the Soviet Union. The Soviets were the defending world champions and they had big talented players such as 7'2" center Arvidas Sabonis and 6'9" forward Alexander Volkov. On their way to the finals of the world championships that summer, the Soviets had won nine games by scoring an average of 107 points per game. The U.S. team, which had won eight games on its way to the final, knew that it wouldn't be easy to beat the Soviets.

As expected, the championship game was full of suspense. The U.S. team twice took a 10-point lead in the first half, but both times the Soviets stormed back. David, who had just learned how to play man-to-man defense, worked hard to keep the dangerous Sabonis in check. Tyrone Bogues, the U.S. team's tiny 5'3" guard, bamboozled the Soviets by stealing the ball 10 times. At the end of the game, guard Valdis Valters took a pass and set up for a tying shot. But Bogues forced him to shoot off-balance. Valters missed and the U.S. captured the gold medal with an 87-85 win. David, who had scored 20 points in the game, celebrated with his teammates. The loss to Duke seemed very far away.

When David returned to the Academy the following fall, he heard some encouraging news. Napoleon McCallum, a star running back for the Navy football team, had been drafted by the Los Angeles Raiders of the National Football League that summer. Napoleon had been stationed in Long Beach, California, near the Raiders' training camp, and the Navy had given him permission to play football on Sundays.

This meant that David might also be given a chance to play for an NBA team while he served in the Navy. "It might help people here accept my playing if they can accept Napoleon playing," David told reporters. "As far as the Navy getting something out of me, I feel it's getting more out of me playing basketball than if I was sitting behind some desk in some room with nobody thinking about me. I am positive publicity for the Navy, and I can see the Navy benefiting from that."

In David's senior season, he had the chance to become the first major college player ever to score more than 2,500 points, grab more than 1,400 rebounds, and sink more than 60 percent of his field-goal attempts. When reporters asked if he was going to concentrate only on basketball, David replied, "I'd have to blow off a lot of things. I could just get by in class, I'm sure. But I'm not sure I can do that and live with myself."

David had plenty of distractions that fall. Some were good. He had a serious girlfriend who was a junior at George Mason University. He was also receiving lots of fan mail, especially from kids who wrote to say that they wanted to be like him. David tried to use his stardom positively by visiting local schools to talk about the dangers of drugs.

Then there were more difficult kinds of distractions. Reporters and photographers requested time with David so often that he was forced to give interviews only one day each week. Fans recognized him instantly wherever he went and they crowded around to ask for his autograph.

Being famous isn't always easy, as David learned. "I spent more time with other people when I was a freshman," he said. "Now it's hard for me to find time just to be alone. I took my privacy for granted. You take a lot of things for granted, like going to the mall and having nobody recognize you. A lot of times you don't want the recognition. It's funny to go places and all of a sudden people recognize me."

Just about the only place where David wasn't treated like a big star was at the Academy. There he was just another midshipman, especially in the eyes of the officers. "It's easy for outsiders to think a guy like this is treated special," said Captain Albert Konetzni, the Deputy Commandant of the Academy. "But David cuts no slack around here. He is perhaps the best ballplayer in the country, but I or anyone else in my command have no problem saying, 'David, sit down, shut up, and do what I say.' I chewed him out for the way his shoes were unshined. We work this kid hard."

Last, but certainly not least, David had to deal with his growing desire to play pro basketball. Not knowing if the Navy would make him wait for five years after graduation was tough. "Last year, I was up in the air about the pros, but yes, I want to play now," he said. "God gave me the height and ability to play and I want to, very much. If I had known two years ago that I would feel this way now, I probably would have made a different decision and not stayed here."

David's desire to play in the NBA as soon as possible touched off a big debate — should military academies treat athletes differently or should they require them to serve for as long as other students?

Many people had opinions on the subject. John Clune, a Navy basketball star from the 1950's, said, "You've got to treat everyone the same. While you can't give the athlete special treatment because he's an athlete, you also can't treat him differently than you would any other student because he's well-known."

Some of David's classmates taunted him for wanting to leave the Navy early. And even the people who sympathized with David were careful not to give the impression that the Academy had two sets of rules for its students. Captain Konetzni said, "If he wasn't a basketball player, I'd say to David, 'You've grown five inches since you've been here. You're not being commissioned (given the rank of officer). Here's your diploma. Bye-bye.' But I want David to serve and I'm sure he wants that, too."

When reporters asked David's dad for his opinion, Mr. Robinson replied, "Let's face it. Midshipmen go to the Academy to be officers and gentlemen. David went there precisely to become that. He stayed for the same reasons he entered. He just happened to turn into a terrific basketball player and give the Navy national recognition. Shouldn't there be some consideration for that?"

While the Navy considered David's future, David concentrated on the upcoming basketball season. Coach Evans had left the Navy over the summer to become head coach of the basketball team at the University of Pittsburgh. Pete Herrmann, who had been the Navy assistant coach, replaced Evans as head coach. Navy was scheduled to play a lot of tough teams and Coach Herrmann and the Midshipmen were counting on David as they never had before. Vernon Butler and Kylor Whitaker had graduated and it was very likely that opposing teams would use three players to guard David the way Duke had done in the NCAA tournament. He would have to be on top of his game.

David knew what lay ahead and he made an extra effort to improve, especially on defense. "When I say defense, I mean being quick on my feet, guarding my man, not letting him drive past me, always knowing where he is," David said. "There are things I need to work on. My goal is to get beyond just using my height. I'm working on my concentration, on being more consistent, on just being tough. Really tough."

David quickly learned how tough he would have to be when Navy opened the season against North Carolina State in the Hall of Fame Tip-Off Classic in Springfield, Massachusetts. (Springfield is where the basketball Hall of Fame is located.) He played sluggishly in the first half and the Midshipmen quickly fell behind. By the time he got going, they were trailing by 16 points early in the second half.

Suddenly, David exploded. He poured in 20 points in a little more than nine minutes and Navy began to catch up. Unfortunately, David played a little too tough on defense. He was called for his fifth foul and had to leave the game with 1:23 left to play. Navy was leading 83-82, at the time. Then Kenny Drummond of N.C. State sank a three-point field goal with 14 seconds left on the clock. When the buzzer sounded, N.C. State had sunk the Midshipmen, 86-84.

The loss made David angry even though he had set Tip-Off Classic records for most points scored (36), most points scored in one half (26), and most field goals (14). After the game, he apologized to his teammates by saying, "Good players help their teams win. All the points in the world don't matter if you lose."

David redeemed himself the following week by coming to Navy's rescue against Michigan State. The game had gone into overtime after Michigan State tied the score with a three-point shot at the final buzzer. David gave Navy a 91-90 win by taking a pass from guard Bobby Jones, turning, and sinking a 10-foot shot. His final total of 43 points was the most he had ever scored in a single game.

Coach Evans had come back to watch the game and was impressed by the way David had taken charge. "It seems as if David's matured a lot," he said. "From what I've seen and heard, his attitude is excellent. I think he may still have a tendency to loaf when he doesn't feel challenged, but, man, when he turns it on, he is awesome. He can be anything he wants to be. He can survive anything he wants to survive."

David admitted that there were times when he had trouble getting up during games and he thought he knew why. "To tell the truth, I find it a little harder to get going because Coach Herrmann doesn't yell at me," he commented. "Paul Evans uses negative leadership a lot. He'd yell at us, call us names. Every halftime he had something to say. I think I was motivated a little by Coach Evans because he would make me mad and I would go out there and do it. Now I have to trigger myself."

Triggering himself became a mighty chore in early January after the Navy told David that a decision was about to be made on his service commitment. The Navy was considering shortening his length of service to two years, but there was no guarantee that they would. David began to worry about his chances of becoming a pro player.

While he waited for Navy's decision, David found that it was almost impossible to concentrate in class or on the basketball court. He appeared sluggish in practice and he scored only eight points in a 64-62 loss to Richmond the night before the decision was to be announced.

Even though David was recruited by many colleges, his father encouraged him to enter the Naval Academy. The Robinsons impressed upon their children the importance of education and dedication to the pursuit of success. David's father, Ambrose; his younger brother, Chuck; David; his older sister, Kimberly; and his mother, Freda, remain very close, despite all the time David spends on the road with the Spurs.

Lieutenant (junior grade) David Robinson was the tallest player in Naval Academy history. En route to a degree in engineering, David became known as "The Aircraft Carrier" on the basketball court and packed the stands at Navy home games.

Committed to becoming the greatest Navy basketball player ever, David led his team to within one game of the 1986 NCAA Final Four. He was tough under the boards in the Eastern Regionals, but Navy lost to Duke University, 71-50, and its remarkable season ended.

In addition to tackling tough courses such as physics, computer science, and advanced calculus, David learned engineering and navigation aboard ships and submarines.

David was head and shoulders above the crowd during his senior year at Navy as he led his team to a 30-5 record and another appearance in the NCAA championship tournament.

Jamming for two, David propelled the U.S. to victory in the 1986 World Basketball Championships in Spain the summer before his senior year. At the beginning of his final season at Navy, David was the most celebrated college basketball player in the country. He went on to win College Basketball Player of the Year honors.

Manny Millan/Sports Illustrated

David tried to keep the ball out of Brazil's reach during the Pan Am Games in 1987. But his work for the Navy at Kings Bay, Georgia, left little time for basketball practice. David played poorly overall, and the U.S. lost the gold medal to Brazil.

At the 1988 Olympics in Seoul, David was expected to soar and lead the U.S. team to gold. Instead, he did not play well and the team finished a disappointing third.

Many people felt that David Robinson's incredible talent would not survive a two-year stint in the Navy. But David was chosen first overall by San Antonio in the 1987 NBA draft and the long wait began. In 1989, trades and draft picks gave coach Larry Brown, (above, left) a redesigned team, and David was the final piece in the puzzle. By the time the preseason began, David was the hottest topic in basketball. Many people felt that David wouldn't be able to make it in the NBA. But Larry Brown had faith in his center, and after an impressive exhibition season, the stage was set for one of the most dominant rookie performances in NBA history.

November 4, 1989 marked David Robinson's debut in the NBA as he squashed doubts about his ability. David's stellar performance against the Lakers allowed the Spurs to pull a stunning upset, 106-98.

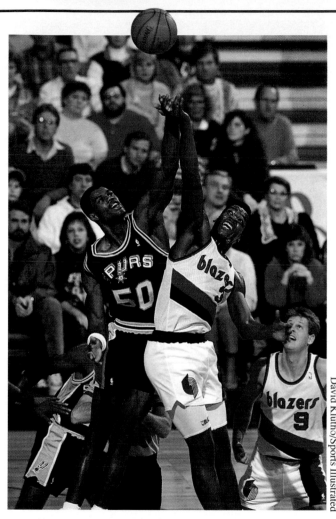

Because he is 7'1", David has an extraordinary ability to swat the ball away from others. In college, he set an NCAA record for most blocked shots in a game (14) and in a season (207).

By taking a synthesizer keyboard with him on road trips, David is always ready to write music. He and teammate Terry Cummings (left) recently recorded a song together.

The Last 10 Rookies of the Year

1989-90 — **David Robinson, San Antonio**

1988-89 — Mitch Richmond, Golden State

1987-88 — Mark Jackson, New York

1986-87 — Chuck Person, Indiana

1985-86 — Patrick Ewing, New York

1984-85 — Michael Jordan, Chicago

1983-84 — Ralph Sampson, Houston

1982-83 — Terry Cummings, San Diego

1981-82 — Buck Williams, New Jersey

1980-81 — Darrell Griffith, Utah

DAVID ROBINSON, NOW AN NBA STAR, ALMOST DIDN'T PLAY PROFESSIONALLY. IN RETURN FOR HIS EDUCATION, DAVID PROMISED TO STAY IN THE NAVY FOR FIVE YEARS AFTER GRADUATION. WOULD ANY PRO TEAMS WAIT?

AS A JUNIOR, DAVID LED THE TEAM TO ITS FIRST NCAA TOURNAMENT APPEARANCE SINCE 1960. HE THOUGHT ABOUT TRANSFERRING TO ANOTHER SCHOOL TO GET TO THE PROS FASTER.

REMEMBER, DAVID, THERE'S MORE TO LIFE THAN BASKETBALL.

BEFORE DECIDING, KEEP IN MIND THAT THE ACADEMY CAN PREPARE YOU FOR ANYTHING YOU WANT TO DO!

IN JANUARY OF DAVID'S SENIOR YEAR, THE NAVY REDUCED HIS COMMITMENT TO TWO YEARS BECAUSE IT WAS FELT THAT HE WOULD HELP ATTRACT OTHER GOOD ATHLETES TO THE ACADEMY IF HE WERE ALLOWED TO PLAY IN THE NBA. THEN THERE WAS THE FACT THAT HE WAS TOO TALL TO FIT IN SUBMARINES, SHIPS, OR PLANES.

NOW YOU HAVE TO WORRY ABOUT STAYING IN SHAPE FOR THE NBA!

YES. TWO YEARS IS A LONG TIME TO BE AWAY FROM THE GAME.

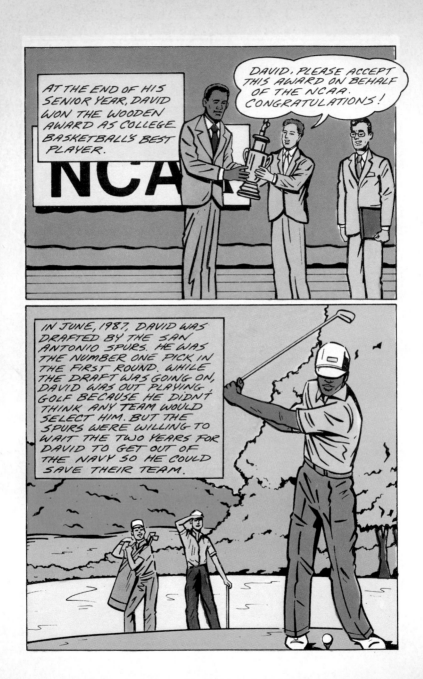

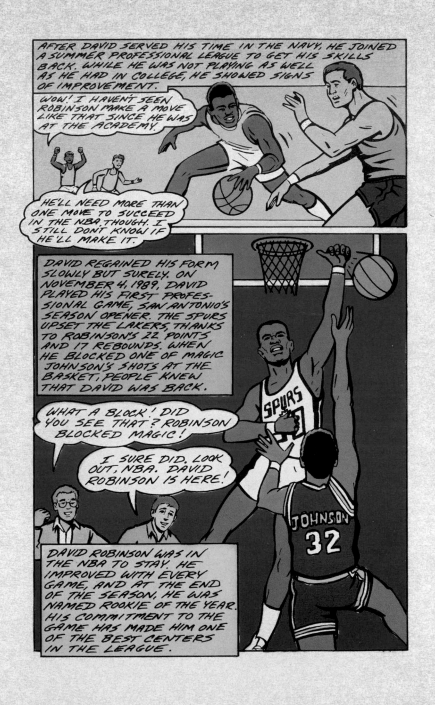

"David was a wreck," Hootie Liebert says. "You could tell during the game that his mind was nowhere near the court. He knew the decision was coming the next day and that was all he could think about. That night, he said, 'They may make me stay the whole five years.' He was scared."

David's fears vanished on January 9, 1987, when Navy Secretary John Lehman announced that David would only have to serve two years after graduation. During that time he would be permitted to play in the 1987 Pan Am Games and the 1988 Summer Olympics. After that he would be required to serve four years in the Naval Reserves, where he would report for training three weeks each summer.

David was relieved when he heard the news. "Two years is better than five years," he said to reporters. "I'm glad it's over and I know what my future is going to be. I've probably been more ruffled the last three days than I've ever been. I figured that the Navy would be fair and consider what's best for me and what's best for the Navy. I feel like that's pretty much what happened."

The Navy decided that David would help them most by serving as an example of what a person could do if he or she chose to attend the Academy. "If you talk about the basketball program, then kids think that it might be an interesting place to go," David says. "Then they look at the academic side and they see that it's really good. Then they think, 'Wow, I can play basketball and get a good education. That's pretty neat.'"

To be an effective spokesman for the Navy, David would need an opportunity to play. The Pan Am Games and Olympics would give him just that opportunity. Then he would still have a chance to be drafted by an NBA team.

David's chances of playing in the NBA looked very good. Like Napoleon McCallum, David would be allowed to play professionally on a part-time basis during his two years of active service. However, that would be possible only if he was drafted by a team near the base where he was stationed. Many officials from NBA teams said they would be happy to draft David even if it meant he could only play part-time for the first two years.

"We'd build a Naval station on top of Madison Square Garden if we could get him," remarked Dick McGuire, a scout for the New York Knicks.

David didn't mind the idea of playing part-time in the NBA, but he also knew it would be hard to keep his skills sharp while he worked at a full-time job in the Navy.

"Basketball is definitely a full-time job," he said. "It's tough to do both. I think the NBA team would get me used to the scenery, the whole life-style, for two years. I don't think they would worry about me contributing that much. They would be priming me for when I get out."

The Navy's decision to shorten David's service commitment was not a completely popular one. Newspapers around the country printed editorials and letters from readers disagreeing with the idea that athletes should be given special treatment by military academies. The biggest complaint was that David had made an agreement when he entered the Academy to serve in the Navy for five years after graduation. In return, he had been given an education that was paid for by money that came from people's income taxes. Many people felt that David should pay back taxpayers by honoring his service agreement.

David expected people to feel that way. "Some people are going to be upset," he said, "but half the people are going to be glad for me because they feel I'm gifted and that it's not my fault that I've grown."

After David learned that he would only have to serve

for two years, he celebrated by scoring 45 points and grabbing 21 rebounds in a 95-70 win over James Madison. It was
easier to focus on basketball again.

Night after night, David worked his magic. On January
25, he scored 45 points against Kentucky in a game shown
on national TV. Even though Navy lost, 80-69, David
received a standing ovation from Kentucky's fans. Six days
later, he led Navy to a heart-pounding win over North
Carolina-Wilmington, in which he launched a 16-foot fade-
away shot that beat the buzzer to give Navy a 67-66 victory.

Five nights later, David made the most dazzling play
of his career. This time Navy was trailing James Madison,
71-70, with only two seconds left to play. Coach Herrmann
diagrammed a play that would give David a chance to take
one final shot at the basket.

The air was heavy with tension when play resumed.
Doug Wojcik got the ball and fired it downcourt to David.
The pass was high and it looked like it was going to sail over
his head. At the last second, David ran under it, stretched
out, reached high, and caught the ball at the midcourt line.
In one smooth motion, he pulled the pass in and shot. The
ball sailed toward the basket, but seemed to be fading too

far to the left. The players and the crowd held their breath as the ball hit the backboard and bounced into the net! Navy won 73-71. The crowd exploded and David was mobbed by his teammates, who carried him off the court.

By the time Navy played its arch-rival, Army, on February 21, the Midshipmen had steamed to a 21-5 record. David was the third-leading scorer in college basketball with a 28.7 points-per-game average.

The game against Army was special because it was the last home game that David, Hootie Liebert, and Doug Wojcik would play for Navy. Halsey Field House was packed with a sellout crowd, and the Midshipmen carried flowers onto the court to give to the families of the players who were graduating at the end of the year. It was an emotional moment for everyone in attendance that night.

David had to fight to keep Navy together during the tough game that followed. Three defenders hounded him during the first half and he scored only eight points. It wasn't until late in the second half that David finally broke loose. He scored six of Navy's last seven points on a dunk, a turnaround jumper, and two free throws as the Midshipmen won a squeaker, 58-52.

Navy went on to win its third conference championship in a row and earn another appearance in the NCAA tournament. David was chosen once again as the conference's player of the year. In the weeks that followed, David was given the Naismith Award, the Eastman Award, the Wooden Award, and the Rupp Trophy, all for being selected as the College Basketball Player of the Year by various organizations and groups of sportswriters. The Associated Press named David to its College All-America First Team. Of the five players selected, David was the only one to receive a vote from each of the 10 basketball writers who chose the team.

"It has been a fairy-tale story for me," David commented during one interview. "I wasn't expecting much from basketball when I came to Navy, maybe a little recreation. It's been a great thrill for me learning this game, developing some appreciation for it, disciplining myself through the Navy experience to get better at it."

On March 12, 1987, David played his final game for Navy. That day the Midshipmen took on Michigan in the first round of the NCAA tournament. The game was played in Charlotte, North Carolina, and David set a Navy record by scoring 50 points. He also pulled down 13 rebounds, but it wasn't enough for a victory. Navy lost 97-82.

When David was taken out of the game with only a few seconds left to play, the crowd stood and cheered. "I felt kind of like Michael Jordan," David says, "because he always gets great hands at home or on the road."

After the game, Michigan's coach Bill Frieder, saluted the Navy's greatest player of all time by saying, "He's a great, great player. The best college player I've seen in my seven years as a coach and that includes Patrick Ewing."

In the Navy locker room, David told his teammates: "No matter where I go or what I do the rest of my life, I'll never forget you guys. If you ever need anything, don't be afraid to come to me and ask for help."

David's wonderful career in college basketball was over at last. "It hasn't hit me yet, but I'm sure it will," he told reporters. "The lights are out, the hype is over, the cheers have subsided. Those things come and go. It's the friend-ships with my teammates that I'll cherish forever. They are the kinds of things that I'll carry with me the rest of my life."

David paused and thought of all that he had done. "It's been a long road," he said. "I've learned to love the game."

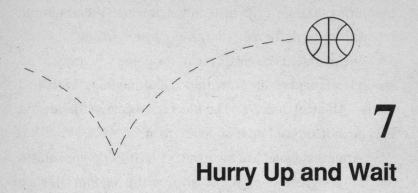

7

Hurry Up and Wait

After the 1987 NCAA tournament, David returned to the Academy to relax and catch up on his schoolwork. His grade point average had slipped that year from 3.3 to 2.8 out of a possible 4.0 and David had heard about it. "My mother is all over me because of that," he said.

David heard some good news, too — he was certain to be the first college player chosen in the NBA draft that June. "There is no doubt that David Robinson will be the Number 1 draft pick," announced TV broadcaster Dick Vitale. "I don't care what his service requirements are. He is the total package, a franchise player."

Even though David would only be able to play part-time in the NBA for the next two years, most teams were still eager to have him. He was by far the most talented player available in that year's draft.

But it began to look as though David's entry into the pros would take longer than he had expected. On March 26, it was reported that James H. Webb, Junior, who was about to become the new Secretary of the Navy, did not want Navy athletes to play pro sports until their service commitments were over. "I believe taxpayers who contribute $130,000 to educate each midshipman deserve the full value for their money," Webb later said. "Those who accept such assistance should understand that being an officer is a 24-hour a day job."

There was now a good chance that David would not join the NBA, even part-time, until his two-year commitment was over.

On April 1, David was honored at a dinner at the Los Angeles Athletic Club where he received the John Wooden Award as the 1987 College Basketball Player of the Year. Reporters asked him what he thought the Navy would do. "My future is a cloudy crystal ball right now," he replied. "All I know is what I read in the papers, like the rest of you."

On April 14, David found out what the Navy would do. Navy Secretary Webb decided that Navy athletes, including David and Napoleon McCallum, would not be allowed to play pro sports until they completed their service commitments. It was a terrible blow for Napoleon, who had four years left to serve. As for David, he would still be allowed to play in the Pan Am Games and the Olympics, but he could not join an NBA team until 1989.

Reporters wanted to know how David felt, but he was too busy taking final exams to talk to them. Not being able to play pro basketball for two years was actually going to turn out to be to David's advantage. He could now choose the NBA team he wanted to join. If he did not want to sign with the team that drafted him that June, he could wait a year and enter the draft again. If he was still not chosen by a team he liked, he could wait yet another year. At that point, he would be eligible to sign with any team.

David did not have any particular team in mind, but people talked about how awesome he would look playing for the Bulls with Michael Jordan or for the Lakers with Magic Johnson. "It's a great option to say that two years from now, I can play with whomever I want," David told reporters. "The big factor is my comfort level. Wherever you go, there's going to be something you don't like."

One thing David didn't like was losing. Sportswriters were sure that he would rather play for a winning team like the Lakers or the Boston Celtics instead of one of the weaker teams that would draft him that year or the next. "You look at the Lakers and they're in the finals every year," David said. "It would be great to win 60 games a year."

There is a famous sports saying that goes: "Winning isn't everything, it's the only thing." In David's case, happiness was the only thing. "I talked to a couple of guys on the Lakers and they seemed pretty happy," he said. "But I knew some good teams in college that were not happy playing together. To me, that's important."

On May 17, the NBA held its annual draft lottery. The seven teams with the worst records the previous season (the New York Knicks, New Jersey Nets, Cleveland Cavaliers, Phoenix Suns, Los Angeles Clippers, Sacramento Kings, and San Antonio Spurs) were entered in a random drawing. The team that was drawn first would pick first in the draft. Of course, that pick would be David.

The Spurs were so eager to draft David that they held

a "Lucky Charm" contest. Fans were asked to send in an object that would bring good luck at the lottery. One fan, Roberto Pachecano, sent a tie that had a red chameleon and the Spurs' team colors, silver and black, on the clasp. Pachecano, whose father had been a sailor, said that red chameleons were supposed to bring good luck to seamen. "Lore has it that if shipwrecked sailors found a red chameleon, they would survive," he said.

In a way, the Spurs were shipwrecked and hoping to survive. They had suffered through a 28-54 record the previous season, their second losing year in a row. Attendance at their home games had been so poor, they were in danger of being moved to another city. The red chameleon tie seemed appropriate because David was a Navy man, so the Spurs gave Pachecano a free trip to New York City to see the draft lottery drawing. Sure enough, the first team drawn was the Spurs!

"There's no doubt in my mind that we will draft David," said Bob Bass, the Spurs general manager. "He's a terrific athlete who's 7'1" and a young player who hasn't scratched the surface of his ability. When he gets with better players, he'll be even better."

Actually, David was already with better players. He was in Colorado Springs trying out for the U.S. Basketball Team that would play in the Pan American Games that summer. Among the other college stars who were trying out were forward Danny Manning of Kansas, guard Rex Chapman of Kentucky, and guard Pooh Richardson of UCLA. All three are now playing in the NBA. David says scrimmaging against them, especially Manning, "really opened my eyes and improved my game."

David made the team and returned to the Academy for graduation. On May 20, he received a degree in math and computer science and his commission as an ensign in the United States Navy. At the end of the ceremony, David and all the other new ensigns let out a cheer and happily threw their hats in the air.

Two weeks later, David was assigned to the Kings Bay submarine base in Georgia, where he would serve as the Assistant Resident Officer in Charge of Construction. He would be paid $315.23 a week to supervise the building of docks and service facilities for submarines. The Navy told him to report for duty on June 19.

On June 22, the NBA draft was held in New York City.

To no one's surprise, the Spurs made David the first player chosen. It was an exciting but scary time for San Antonio because there was no guarantee that David would agree to play for the Spurs.

On the day of the NBA draft, David was in Washington D.C., where he visited Vice President Bush at the White House and played in a celebrity golf tournament with entertainer Bob Hope. David was on the golf course when he was told that he had been drafted by the Spurs. Later on, reporters asked if he wanted to play for them.

"The Spurs have to show they have the will to make their team better in the next few years, that the players are happy there, and that the fans will come out and support the team," he replied. "I hope to go down to San Antonio and look around, get to know the organization and see the people in charge. I don't want to make any decision right away. I just want to relax and enjoy my experience in the Navy."

In mid-July, David took a break from his duties at Kings Bay and reported to Team USA's training camp in Louisville, Kentucky. He agreed to keep a daily diary about his experiences for *The Washington Post* newspaper. He was impressed with his teammates, according to an August entry:

"Practice, in fact, is two-and-a-half hours of highlight film. It's been the most exciting thing because there is so much talent, so much endless energy."

But David's teammates did not think that he seemed very excited. "You hear all the talk about the Player of the Year and you expect him to be a killer at practice," said guard Keith Smart. "After a couple of days, we realized that he just wasn't a practice player. The thing is, even at half speed, he dominated the practice."

Team USA prepared for the Pan Am Games, which would begin on August 9 in Indianapolis, Indiana, with three weeks of intra-squad scrimmages. Team USA was heavily favored to win the Pan Am gold medal. In the tournament's 36-year history, the U.S. had won 47 games and lost only twice while capturing eight gold medals in nine tries. David was confident he and his teammates would carry on that winning tradition. "I don't think there are a lot of teams that can stop us," he said.

Team USA opened the Pan Am Games against Panama. It was a hard-fought contest that sometimes resembled a brawl. David was constantly pushed and shoved by Panama's bruising center, Mario Butler, who was 6'8" and weighed 225 pounds. Team USA lost two players to injuries inflicted by Panama's physical players. But while David struggled against Butler, Danny Manning put Panama away with a great display of passing and timely shooting. Manning scored 18 points and Team USA won 91-63.

David told a reporter for *The New York Times* how Panama's toughness had caught his team off guard: "We came out kind of ready mentally, but not really ready for the physical nature of the game. I think we were surprised at how strong they were. I know that I was working hard and wasn't doing the things I'm supposed to do. Tomorrow we have to come out ready to play, not just with our skulls, but with our bodies, too."

Unfortunately, it did not appear that David was ready to play in the next game. He scored only 10 points and grabbed 7 rebounds in an 85-58 victory over Argentina. Team USA's defense sparked the win by forcing 16 turnovers and holding Argentina to only two three-pointers in the first 13 1/2 minutes of the second half.

After the game reporters asked, "What's wrong with David?" Coach Crum replied, "David's probably not in as good a shape as some of the other players. He's not getting a chance to show his true form. You'll see two or three players hanging on him every time the ball goes to him. It's going to be hard for him."

It wasn't until the semi-final game, against Puerto Rico, that David finally busted loose. He scored 20 points and shut down Puerto Rico's best player, José Ortiz, who led all scorers in the game with 31 points. Ortiz scored 22 of them in the first half, but then David went to work.

In one play, David batted Ortiz's shot back into his face. Ortiz shot again. David swatted it away. Ortiz got the ball back and shot again. David grabbed the rebound. It was the kind of defensive play David was famous for, and he was relieved that he had finally come through for his teammates.

"They needed more from me than they'd been getting," David told reporters. "The previous two games, I'd only gotten nine rebounds per game and 12 points. I feel I'm in good shape. I just haven't played as much as everyone else. Kings Bay is a real small town and there's nowhere within an hour's drive that I can play competitive basketball."

Unfortunately, Team USA did not get much from David in the gold medal game against Brazil. David quickly picked up three fouls and had to play less aggressively. Two more and he would have had to leave the game. Brazil's Oscar Schmidt took advantage of the situation and scored 46 points.

Team USA had a 15-point lead with 17 minutes left to play when David went up for a rebound. He was bumped and fell backward. When he grabbed the rim of the basket to steady himself, he was whistled for a fourth foul. Coach Crum then took David out to save him for the final minutes, in case the game went down to the wire.

As David sat on the bench, Brazil fought back to take a one-point lead. There was still 7:41 left to play, but Coach Crum decided it was time to put his best defender back in. About a minute later, David went to block a shot. The referee thought David made contact with the opposing player and whistled a fifth foul. David was out of the game. With David gone, Brazil surged ahead and won the game, 120-115, and the gold medal.

"This is far worse than losing to Duke," David wrote in his diary for *The Washington Post*. "Duke was expected to win. Our Pan Am team was absolutely expected to win and didn't. I knew Brazil was capable of beating us, but I never expected to lose. One of the worst feelings an athlete can have is knowing his teammates need him and not being able to do anything about it."

David took the loss especially hard because he knew he would not be able to play again for a long time. But his spirits were given a lift in September when the Spurs sent a private plane to fly him, his parents, his brother, Chuck, and his agent to San Antonio. The small city of 786,000 people in south-central Texas rolled out the red carpet. About 700 fans greeted David when he arrived at the airport. Many held signs that said SAY YES, DAVID.

During the next three days, David took a helicopter tour of the city and went to a country club where he played golf with his dad and team president Angelo Drossos. He met with the city's mayor, Henry Cisneros, and attended dinner parties. Alvin Robertson and Johnny Dawkins of the Spurs took him to nightclubs.

"I'm trying to stay neutral, but it's hard to hold back," David said at a packed news conference with Mayor Cisneros. "It's great to be wanted. It's hard to hold back that smile and say, 'Thank you.' From what I've seen of this city, this is a fantastic place and we love it here. I have a lot to think about. It's going to take a while to mull it over."

One thing he had to think about was playing for a losing team. David knew he would face a lot of pressure because fans would expect him single-handedly to make the Spurs a winner. "I don't want to be put in a situation like that," he told sportswriter Gordon Edes of *The Los Angeles Times*. "I believe I can be a very, very good player. But I don't want people to expect I can come down here and move mountains. It's not that easy."

Bob Bass, the Spurs general manager, promised that he was working hard to make the team better. "We made a commitment that we needed to rebuild the club," he said. "We have six or seven young players, and David Robinson is another piece of the puzzle. It's extremely important to this franchise to sign him."

Once again David had a big decision to make, but this one was much more fun. "I've already had to make some tough, hard decisions, but this one is fantastic," he said. "Either way, you can't go wrong."

That fall people talked constantly about what David would do. Many were convinced he would turn San Antonio down and later sign with the Lakers or the Celtics.

On November 5, Hootie Liebert, David's former roommate at Navy, told *The San Antonio Express-News* that David wanted to play for the Spurs. "David called me tonight and told me he will be wearing the black and silver of the Spurs," Hootie said. "David told me, 'They have done everything to make me happy. They have been honest and fair with me. How can I turn it down?'"

The next day, David and his parents went to the HemisFair Arena in San Antonio where about 500 fans watched him sign his contract. It was a great day for the city and its team, and one that David's family never envisioned when he was a teenage computer whiz who didn't even like basketball. Or even more recently than that. "If you had told me a year ago that this would happen, I wouldn't have believed it," said David's dad. "I wouldn't have believed it six months ago, even two months ago."

David's contract made him the highest paid athlete in team sports. He was given $26 million to play for the Spurs for eight years, plus a two million dollar bonus just for signing the contract! But the money he received wasn't the reason he agreed to play for San Antonio.

"There's no amount of money I would have signed for if they did not have a commitment to making this franchise better," David commented. "I decided this was the place I wanted to be."

The day after he signed his contract, David and his dad went to HemisFair Arena to watch the Spurs play the Dallas Mavericks. David had to be encouraged by what he saw. The Spurs won 130-106! The game also made him eager to begin his new career.

"He wants to play now, so he is very edgy," his dad said. "The hardest thing of all for David is the waiting."

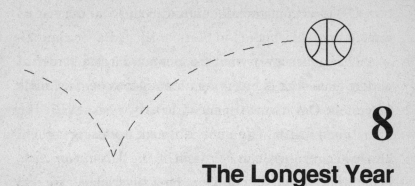

8

The Longest Year

Basketball took a back seat to David's naval duties at Kings Bay during the winter of 1987-88. He worked each day from 8 AM to 4 PM in a trailer that served as his office. His job was to make sure construction projects at the base were finished on time and that the workmen were paid.

"It was something I had never done before, sitting behind a desk all day," David remembers. "We went through great amounts of paper, making sure the construction companies had safety plans, environmental plans, insurance plans. There were always papers to write and reports to do. I had to understand the construction, so I had to do a lot of homework."

David lived in a condominium about 35 miles away on Amelia Island Plantation in Florida. Kings Bay is approximately 10 miles away from the Georgia-Florida border. A sliding glass door in his living room opened onto the ninth hole of the Oak March Country Club.

"I'm living in two entirely different worlds right now," David told reporter John Feinstein of *The Washington Post*. "One world, I rule. It's all there on a silver platter for me. People want to give me an incredible amount of money to play a game, to do something I enjoy. That boggles my mind. In the other world, I'm at the bottom of the totem pole. I might be asked to run out and get coffee for people. The whole situation is teaching me a lot. I'm learning about power and about restraint."

He was also learning about wealth and fame. "It's a funny thing how people who have everything can always get more," David told Feinstein. "When you don't have anything, you can't catch a break. I've thought about that a lot. A few weeks ago, before I signed the contract, I was in a Burger King. The manager said to me, 'Hey, after you sign and you're rich and famous, come back and we'll give you some free food.' That's typical. A guy who isn't rich could use that free food. Once you're rich, why do you need free food? But that's when people want to give it to you."

The Navy also gave David plenty to learn. During the time he was stationed at Kings Bay, he was sent to Port Hueneme, California, for two months to attend eight hours of civil engineering classes each day. He also visited schools to talk to kids about the Academy and the dangers of drugs.

With so much to do, David had little time to stay in shape. He lifted weights and ran. Occasionally, he practiced with Jacksonville University's basketball team. He did not get a chance to play until March, when the Armed Forces Tournament was held at Camp Lejeune in North Carolina. By then, David was itching to play.

"When I watch TV or go to a game, it's hard," he said. "I don't get the chance to get on the court and express myself the way I like to."

David wanted to use the Armed Forces Tournament as a tune-up for the Olympic team tryouts in May. It was clear that he needed one. In his first game with the all-Navy team, David scored 13 points, grabbed 7 rebounds, and blocked 6 shots, but he also dropped several passes and missed a bunch of easy shots.

"I didn't expect much tonight and I was right," he said after the game. "All I wanted to do was run up and down the court and get the feeling of playing back."

The next night, David scored only six points and fouled out in a 118-71 loss to Army. "That was probably my low point," he said. "I need to get in shape. I want to be ready for the Olympic trials. I don't want to go there and be just another player."

David's ragged performance against Army alarmed the coaches of the U.S. Olympic Basketball Team. After the game, assistant coach Bill Stein called head coach John Thompson and said, "David couldn't get down the court three times in a row!"

When David failed to play any better at the Amateur Basketball Association Tournament in April, the Navy decided to give him a hand. He was sent to the Academy for a special training program designed to improve his stamina. For four weeks, David worked out for up to five hours each day. On Monday, Wednesday, and Friday mornings he lifted weights. On Tuesday and Thursday mornings he jogged or swam. Each afternoon, he ran wind sprints and scrimmaged with Navy's basketball team. He was driven hard all the time. "I keep on him," Coach Herrmann said. "I yell, 'It's like high school again, David! You've got to make the team!'"

That was true. As great as David had been, there were no guarantees that he would make the Olympic team, which would be coached by John Thompson, the coach at George-town. "I'd seen John Thompson's teams, and the way they run up and down the floor," David says. "I knew I wasn't going to make the team if I wasn't in any kind of shape."

The Olympic tryouts began on May 15. Coach Thomp-son took David aside. "I told David what I expected of him," he says. "I wasn't sure what to expect when I saw him, but I didn't want to wait until it was too late. I was very pleased with what David said. He wanted to play on the team and is very enthusiastic about the Olympics."

"I want the Olympic gold medal," David said. "I didn't enjoy losing to Brazil in the Pan Am Games last summer."

Practice was tough, but it felt good to be part of a team again. "I think it makes it so much more fun to come out and work with all the guys," David said. "When you're working by yourself, it's hard to keep your spirits up and keep yourself motivated all the time."

In June, Team USA sent David to Europe for two weeks with a group of players who needed extra work. They played in such countries as Finland, France, and Spain. They won all their games easily, although David played poorly. He scored nine points against Holland and England, and only five points against Finland. He was even worse against France, scoring four points and committing four turnovers and four fouls.

His teammates were stunned. "Dave's so rusty and yet he doesn't act like he's into games at all," said guard Steve Kerr. "I don't see how this tour does the rest of us much good, the competition is so ridiculous. But the whole trip was supposed to be for him. That kind of worries us."

David admitted it was hard for him to get up for games against weak opponents. "Traditionally, I've not done well against lesser competition," he said. "But if the tour has helped me at all, it's shown me how far I have to go."

David found his true form at last in a game against Spain, the toughest team the U.S. team faced on the tour. "This is the one you've been waiting for," Coach Raveling told him before the game. Coach Raveling, head coach of USC's basketball team, was an assistant coach of the

Olympic team and the head coach of this traveling team, known as the "U.S. Selects." David responded with his old rim-rattling dunks and soft turnaround jumpers. He scored 18 points and grabbed 9 rebounds in a 109-87 win.

"Geesh," Steve Kerr said after the game, "I guess he just needs somebody good to play against."

In August, David played against even better competition: pickup teams of NBA stars such as Patrick Ewing, Charles Barkley, Chris Mullin, and Chuck Person. Team USA won the first game, 90-82, but David looked tired and played listlessly. Fans and reporters wondered what was wrong with David Robinson.

"The year away set David back," Coach Thompson said. "You have to get that competitive look, get used to the play and the travel all over again. How quickly he comes back depends on David. He's an outstanding talent, but it's not what he talks about, it's what he does. He has to do more work."

That was obvious from the way David played in the third game. He committed two fouls in the first four minutes and had to sit on the bench for much of the first half. He might as well have stayed there. When he went back in, he was pushed around by the NBA players and made a lot of mistakes.

David scored only 13 points as his teammates shook their heads in disbelief. Coach Thompson screamed himself hoarse. "David, grab the ball!" he yelled. "David, get over there! Cut the baseline off!" he hollered as Michael Jordan blew by David for an easy layup.

David was confused and upset with himself. "Everyone has improved dramatically and it's like I haven't improved at all," he said. "I still do a lot of dumb things. There's no time to think, but I'll make a mistake, then spend a couple of minutes thinking about it. The layoff has taken the confidence out of my game. I've just got to keep working hard."

In the team's first six exhibition games, David scored an average of only 9.3 points per game and a measly 6.2 rebounds. Even worse, he committed 11 turnovers and spent a lot of time on the bench because he had gotten into foul trouble.

David's teammates could not believe that this was the same player who had been such a superstar at Navy. Many people doubted that he was as good as they had thought. It was a difficult time, but David hung tough. "To tell the truth,

I don't care what people expect," he said. "I get my motivation from inside, not from whether people say I played well or poorly."

Not everyone had lost faith in David. "I feel even better about him than when we drafted him," Spurs general manager Bob Bass told reporters. "I know there's a lot he's got to do, but I'm not getting discouraged at all."

David also got a vote of confidence from his teammate who didn't make the cut, Stacey King. "David was playing against 6'5" and 6'6" guys in the Armed Forces Tournament," King said. "Now he's going against the best of the best. In practice, he's the same guy I saw play on TV. You wait until the Olympics and I expect David to really burst back onto the scene."

Many of David's problems had to do with learning to play Coach Thompson's style of basketball. At Navy, he was the team's main scoring threat. With Team USA, all players were given an equal chance to score. At Navy, the team played at a slower pace. They walked the ball up the court on offense and played a zone defense. Team USA ran constantly on offense and used a man-to-man defense.

"This type of game is more reaction," David said. "You

don't have time to stop and yell at yourself, or stop and think about what you have to do next. You have to know what to do next. It hasn't come naturally to me yet."

The more David struggled, the more frustrated he became. To make matters worse, Coach Thompson yelled at him constantly. Ordinarily, David would not have minded it very much. Coaches had yelled at him before and he had learned to take it as a sign of encouragement. This time, however, he wasn't sure exactly what Coach Thompson wanted him to do. David's confidence was shaky and the last thing he wanted to hear was constant criticism. "It's a change from what I'm used to," David said. "It's hard, when he thinks you have the talent, because he's on you all the time. You know you can play at this level, but you don't always feel you can do it at all times."

Ready or not, David left for the Summer Olympics in Seoul, South Korea, during the second week of September. So much was expected of him. Team USA was favored to win the gold medal and David was said to be the key to their success. "That's what I expect of myself, too," he said.

Team USA got off to a sizzling start. It whipped Spain, 97-53; beat Canada, 76-70; rolled over Brazil, 102-87; demolished China, 108-57; crushed Egypt, 102-35; and trounced Puerto Rico, 94-57.

David had a big game against Spain, scoring 16 points and snatching 11 rebounds. After that he played inconsistently. It didn't hurt his team because Coach Thompson's strategy was working. All the players were contributing. There was no need for David to do everything by himself.

Team USA did not expect to have such an easy time in the semifinal game against the Soviet Union, even though the U.S. national team had beaten the U.S.S.R. in the world championships two years before. The Soviets were America's biggest rivals in basketball. Only once had an American team failed to win the Olympic gold medal and that was in 1972 when the Soviets knocked the U.S. off, 51-50. The outcome of that game was hotly disputed. With one second left to play and the U.S. ahead 50-49, the timekeeper put three seconds back on the clock after a stoppage in play. That gave the Soviets enough time to make the winning shot.

Unfortunately, this time the Soviets needed no help from the timekeeper. They easily sent the ball upcourt to their star center, Arvydas Sabonis, who kept finding the open man. Rimas Kurtinaitis and Sharunas Marchulenis put up a blizzard of three-point shots. When Team USA tried to force turnovers, Danny Manning quickly got into foul trouble and couldn't play very much. He did not score a single point all game.

By halftime the Soviets were leading 47-37. Team USA regrouped and rallied. Forward J.R. Reid led the charge. Team USA outscored the Soviets 13-1 and closed within two points, 59-57.

Then everything fell apart. Team USA failed to score a field goal for more than five minutes. Their fast break was smothered by the Soviets. Their defense collapsed and the Soviets scored on five easy layups. Then, as the final seconds ticked down, forward Charles Smith drove for an easy basket but stumbled and fell. Team USA lost 82-76.

Some people blamed David for the crushing defeat, even though he had scored 19 points and grabbed 12 rebounds. To them, David had been upstaged by Arvidas Sabonis, who had scored 13 points and grabbed 13 rebounds. Like David, Sabonis had not played very much before the Olympics. Sabonis was recovering from an ankle injury.

"Sabonis, 18 months, no practice," Soviet head coach Alexander Gomelsky said after the game. "My opinion, Sabonis okay because he is great talent."

When reporters asked David what had gone wrong, all he could say was, "We didn't score enough points."

Team USA scored enough points to beat Australia, 78-49, for the bronze medal, but it wasn't much consolation. Coach Thompson was still proud of his team. "I hope the American public is sophisticated enough to credit these kids with the effort they gave," he said afterwards. "I don't want anyone acting ashamed unless he didn't do all he could do."

David knew he did not do all he was capable of doing, but he wasn't ashamed, only disappointed. "It took me a long time to get over it," he says. "That was one of the biggest disappointments of my life. It was especially hard for me because I had nowhere to go to forget. The other players went to the NBA or back to their college teams and could play and forget. I had to sit and think about it."

Sitting and thinking got the best of David. In October, he sent a letter to the Navy Secretary to ask if he could play in the NBA that season. In return, he would serve extra time in the Naval Reserve. His request was denied.

To his credit, David took the decision well. "I respect the Secretary's decision and appreciate the Navy's time and consideration," he told reporters in a written statement. "I've enjoyed my service in the U.S. Navy and look forward to serving the remaining six months of active duty and six years of reserve duty with pride."

It had been a long, frustrating year, but at least the time when David would get the chance to finally prove himself in the NBA was drawing closer.

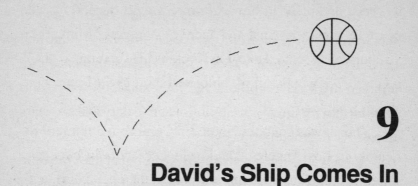

9

David's Ship Comes In

On May 19, 1989, the Navy discharged Lieutenant (Junior Grade) David Robinson from active duty. The demands and challenges of military service were now behind him. Ahead lay the NBA career he had longed for and the challenge of silencing the criticism he had heard since the Olympics.

Many people had been saying that David was overrated and he lacked the intensity and desire to be successful in the NBA. They began having second thoughts that summer.

David decided that the best way to get his game back was by playing in a few of the mid-summer tournaments before practice for the regular season began. At the Midwest

Revue tournament in San Antonio, David burned up the court in games against the Denver Nuggets, Minnesota Timberwolves, and Houston Rockets. He averaged 22.7 points, 8.7 rebounds, and 4.3 blocked shots as the Spurs won all three games.

Then it was on to the Southern California Summer Pro League in Los Angeles. David blocked shots in bunches, stole the ball from opposing players in the open court, and charged like a madman to the basket. He made lob dunks, driving dunks, and monster dunks. Against the Philadelphia 76ers, he jammed home 28 points in the first half and finished with 36 points.

All the while, the new head coach of the Spurs, Larry Brown, looked on with a big smile on his face. Hiring Larry Brown, who had coached the University of Kansas team to the 1988 national championship, was part of the effort by the Spurs to improve the whole team.

David was named the Pro League's MVP, but he wasn't happy. He had still made mistakes and his concentration wandered at times. "I have the potential to be much, much better than that," he said. "I'm a good player right now, but if I approach the game as if there is always something to learn, I can always keep climbing."

"David is going to learn some unbelievable things about himself and the NBA," Coach Brown predicted. "He's pretty critical of himself. He has moments when he plays really hard, but then he doesn't push himself. But I really believe he's going to be terrific."

Obviously, so did the people of San Antonio. On July 25, over 4,000 fans in San Antonio watched with joy as David poured in 31 points, snatched 17 rebounds, and blocked 10 shots in the Spurs' Black-Silver intrasquad game. "I've never seen a guy with that speed and quickness at that size," remarked Bob Bass. "I don't know who to compare him to because there is nobody like him."

After the summer games ended, David spent five hours a day working out at a health club. He stretched, lifted free weights, worked on Nautilus weight machines, strengthened his legs on a climbing machine called the Stairmaster, and played squash and basketball.

"One of the best lessons I learned over the last two years is how to motivate myself," he said. "I couldn't train by myself before. I could train, but not taking myself all the way to the next level until I was numb."

Just before training camp opened on October 6, David received a visit from his former coach at Navy. "Coach Herrmann came to my house and talked to me, tried to give me a little pep talk to get ready," David remembers. "He left and I came back to my refrigerator and on the calendar it had the day October 6 circled. It said, 'Get ready to go with the big boys. '"

David was ready and so were the Spurs. A lot had been done to improve the team in anticipation of David's arrival, in addition to the hiring of Coach Brown. "David is why I'm here," he said. "If David hadn't been here, I wouldn't have come. I would still be at Kansas."

The Spurs had also acquired several good players. In 1988, they drafted guard/forward Willie Anderson, who had played with David in the Olympics. In 1989, they traded for forward Terry Cummings, a seven-year veteran and NBA All-Star. Then they drafted high-scoring forward Sean Elliott of Arizona. In August, they traded for guard Maurice Cheeks who had played in four NBA All-Star games. David was the final piece of the puzzle.

"I was really afraid we wouldn't have a decent team, which is why it was so important to get Terry, Maurice, and

Sean," Coach Brown explained. "With those players, plus Willie Anderson, David doesn't have to worry about scoring. He can direct all his energies to rebounding and defense. He's so fast and quick, he's going to score anyway."

The Spurs were now a much better team than the one that ended the season 21-61 the year before. That team had lost three games by 40 points or more, and had gone an entire month without winning. That wasn't likely to happen again. "I'd be really disappointed if we don't make the playoffs." Coach Brown said. "With the additions we've made, we could be a dangerous team."

Coach Brown drove his talented squad hard in training camp. It didn't matter to him if a player was a big star or not. Everyone had to work.

"Man, Coach Brown is always on me," David said. "You can go out and score 40 points and he'll be furious about 1,000 other things."

Unlike in the past, David was now well-prepared to deal with his coach's vocal fury. "Larry's yelling, now that could get to me if I let it," he said. "But people yelled at me for four years in the Navy, so why get uptight about it? I just sift through what he says and take out the positive. I know he just wants me to be better."

David also knew that all his success at Navy meant nothing now. "When I was in college and winning all those player of the year awards, I said to myself, 'You haven't done anything yet,'" he said. "'You have the pros ahead of you and they're so much bigger and better. All this will be in the past and you'll be starting at zero.' Well, I'm in the pros now and I'm starting from zero. So I'll set goals to strive for, and then when I reach them, I'll keep striving for more."

David began by scoring an average of 22 points in the Spurs' first four pre-season games. In the fifth pre-season game came his first big test. On October 24, he squared off against Patrick Ewing and the New York Knicks at Madison Square Garden. It was an eagerly awaited matchup of talented centers — one of the NBA's best versus the hotshot rookie.

As fans, coaches, and scouts looked on, David and Ewing staged an exciting show of defensive skill. Ewing blocked four shots in the first four minutes. Then David snuffed one of Ewing's dunks as the Spurs held the Knicks to only two points in the first eight minutes. Ewing later broke loose to score 25, but David countered with 22 of his own and the Spurs won the game, 104-99.

When asked by reporters how it felt to beat a player like Patrick Ewing, David said, "I didn't take this as a personal one-on-one battle against Patrick because he has more time in the league, more experience," David replied. "I have so much more to learn about this league. I have to be up every night or I'm going to get pounded. When my head is into it, I still don't think anybody can handle me. But I've got to do that every night. That's what I'm trying to learn now. I've never been through it. It's a long, long season. We'll see how it goes."

When the night of the first regular season game came, David felt sick to his stomach. He was nervous, but he figured that his stomach hurt because of some Mexican food he had eaten. However, many of his teammates weren't feeling too well on opening night, either. "Our young guys were petrified," Coach Brown says. "They were scared to death."

Outside the Spurs locker room, the HemisFair Arena was filled with excitement, hope, and 15,868 people. Magic Johnson, James Worthy, and the rest of the Los Angeles Lakers were waiting in their purple and gold uniforms. The moment of truth had arrived."David's waited a long time for this," Coach Brown said.

"Really, I don't know if San Antonio's fans quite know what to expect from me," David said. "I think they expect me to be a big part of the team's success. I should make the game more exciting for them because I dunk a lot."

Not to mention rebound, pass, and block shots, all of which David did even though he felt like he was going to throw up during most of the first half. Meanwhile, the Spurs played according to plan. Terry Cummings scored 22 points, Maurice Cheeks scored 14, Sean Elliott bagged 16, and Willie Anderson pumped in 12. Together they forced 15 turnovers, out-rebounded the Lakers, 58-39, and stopped Los Angeles's feared fast-break offense in its tracks.

The game was close at first, with the Spurs leading 48-47 at halftime. By then, David felt better and he teamed with Terry Cummings to help San Antonio pull away in the fourth quarter. The Lakers had trimmed the Spurs' lead to 78-72 when David and Terry scored 10 of the Spurs' next 15 points. When the final buzzer sounded, San Antonio had its first win of the season, 106-98.

"It was a great game," Coach Brown said. "Especially

considering the team we had to beat."

Upset stomach and all, David had played wonderfully, leading the Spurs in scoring with 23 points and 17 rebounds. "I haven't seen a guy that big who moves like he does," said Terry Cummings. "He definitely is going to be great."

David had a more cautious opinion about his future. "I think it's a jinx to say I'm going to be great," he said. "I have a lot of potential, but that's not the same as doing it. The main thing is that, finally, I'm getting a chance to play. Now it's up to me."

With Lieutenant (Junior Grade) Robinson in command, the Spurs roared off to win 12 of their first 17 games. He was the team's leading scorer and rebounder nine times during that streak. He lit up New Jersey and the Nets with 26 points in a 109-92 win on December 9th.

Five days later, David played against the great Hakeem Olajuwon and the Houston Rockets for the first time. Just as he had done against Patrick Ewing, David held his own and more. He scored 19 points, snatched 9 rebounds, and frustrated Olajuwon into 7 turnovers. He also kept Houston's superstar center from scoring a point in the final five minutes of the game, which the Spurs won 104-100.

"No question about it," Olajuwon said after the game, "David is a great player."

By January 13, when David scored 27 points in his first regular season game against Patrick Ewing, it was clear that he had improved at an incredible rate.

"Robinson has already done much more than Patrick Ewing ever did in his first year," said Richie Adubato, the head coach of the Dallas Mavericks. "When Patrick came into the league, he was raw and unpolished and he needed a lot of offensive skills. Now Patrick has raised his game and become a force, but it took him three years to do it. David is already a force."

The two tough centers met again on January 17 in San Antonio. Ewing scored 27 points, grabbed 12 rebounds, and blocked 4 shots. David scored 20 points, plucked 6 rebounds, and blocked 3 shots. The score was tied, 90-90, with a minute and 27 seconds left to play when David sank a jump shot over Ewing. Then he flew down the court, stole a pass to Ewing, and started a fast break that put the Spurs up by four points. Finally, with 19 seconds left, Ewing drove in for a score but David blocked Ewing's shot to seal a 101-97 victory.

With that game, there was little doubt that David had joined Patrick and Hakeem as the NBA's best centers. His size, speed, and style of play reminded many people of legendary centers Bill Russell and Wilt Chamberlain. "He runs the floor better than anybody I've seen since Russell," said Basketball Hall of Famer Bob Cousy, who had played with Russell for the Celtics.

David felt honored by such high praise, but as always, he didn't let it go to his head. "When I hear people compare me to Russell, I take pride in it," he said. "They're saying I'm a good player. Russell played a lot of years and was a great player. I'm just starting off."

It had been quite a start. By January 20, David had scored an average of 23 points per game and was the NBA's third leading rebounder (11.4). What's more, he had been named the league's Rookie of the Month each month since the start of the season.

It had also been quite a start for the Spurs. The season was not yet half over, but they had already won 25 games, four more than the previous season. No other team in the league had played so well at home. The Spurs had lost only once at the HemisFair Arena where attendance was up by an average of 3,136 people per game, a team record. They had held their opponents to fewer than 100 points 16 times.

"Our defense is so much better," said Willie Anderson, "but the real key is David."

David was the most talked-about player in the league. He was mobbed by fans in every NBA city and the team bus often had to wait until he finished signing autographs. Sometimes it took David so long that he ended up having to get back to the team's hotel on his own.

Every day reporters crowded around his locker for interviews. They kept talking about the tremendous impact he had had on the Spurs, but David was quick to point out that he wasn't a one-man show. He felt his teammates deserved a great deal of credit. All five starters were averaging at least 10 points per game and their fine play had made his job easier. Without them, he would have been expected to make the Spurs better all by himself.

"It definitely would have been a nightmare for the first year or two," he said. "Nobody really deserves that kind of pressure. These guys are great, especially with their leadership. Caldwell [Jones] knows a little about everybody we've played. He knows what to expect, so everything's not so much of a surprise to me. That's just invaluable. You take away some of those blind obstacles and it makes the path a lot smoother."

Just as David had hoped, the Spurs had become a close group of guys who enjoyed playing and being together. "I feel this is a very good team and that David Robinson is a member of it," he said. "We've developed a lot of pride since the opening game. We've gotten together on the court, and done things off the court. We feel like we're a real good team, and we are getting better. It's something that's real important to us."

One night when the Spurs were in Sacramento, California, David and four teammates went bowling. David had said that he had a 190 average, but the other players didn't believe him. In the first game, David bowled a 125. "Man, were they talking trash after that game," he says.

In the second game, David rolled a 188 even though he couldn't fit his thumb into the ball because his hands were so big. "They wanted a rematch," he says. "I told 'em, 'When are you going to learn?'"

David became best friends with Terry Cummings. Like David, Terry is into music. He has written his own songs and sung on several gospel albums. Sometimes he and David went to a recording studio in San Antonio where they would write music together, sing, or play songs like the "Charlie Brown Theme" or "What a Wonderful World."

Terry also became a valuable teacher who gave David insight on opposing teams and players and tips on how to improve his skills. Best of all, David could count on Terry to come through in games when David wasn't playing well.

"David is tremendous," Terry says. "But the nice thing is he doesn't have to come out and shine every night or even be at his best. He can gradually grow into what he'll be down the road."

"He's going to be a monster," said forward Charles Barkley of the 76ers.

By the All-Star break in February, the monster had led the Spurs to a 32-14 record. No Spurs team had ever done that well in the first half of a season. Naturally, the monster was chosen to play in the All-Star Game and he scored 15 points and grabbed 10 rebounds.

All-Star or not, Coach Brown decided that David was capable of doing even better things, but only if he was pushed harder. What annoyed Coach Brown most was

David's old habit of playing all-out against the tougher teams and coasting against the weaker ones. "Sometimes I just find myself kind of spacing out and not forcing myself to get into the action," David said. "Don't worry, Coach Brown lets me know about it."

With Coach Brown's knee in his back, David rolled through the month of February, averaging 24 points, 12.3 rebounds, 6.9 blocks, and 2 steals in 12 games. In mid-March, he put together a fabulous streak in which he averaged 31.5 points, 13.3 rebounds, and 6 blocks while leading the Spurs to four wins in a row. David's performance earned him NBA Player of the Week honors.

By April, David and the Spurs were a locomotive closing in on the NBA record for the biggest improvement by a team in one year. The record had been set by the Celtics in 1979-80 when a rookie named Larry Bird led the team to 32 more wins than it had had the previous season.

On April 18, the Spurs broke the record by beating the Utah Jazz, 102-93, for their 54th win of the year. The victory was part of a seven-game winning streak that helped San Antonio clinch first place in the Midwest Division.

The NBA had just seen one of the most remarkable

performances by a team and a rookie in the history of the league. David was the unanimous choice of 92 sportswriters and broadcasters for the NBA Rookie of the Year Award. He had led San Antonio in both scoring and rebounding 31 times during the regular season while averaging 24.3 points, 12 rebounds, and 3.9 blocks per game.

David and the Spurs continued their magic season in the playoffs. In the first round, they eliminated the Denver Nuggets in three straight games.

In the second round, the Spurs took on the tough Portland Trail Blazers. It was no cakewalk. The Blazers easily won the first two games on their home court, but the Spurs fought back in San Antonio to tie the series.

In Game Three, David gunned home 28 points to spark a 121-98 rout. Then, in Game Four, he kept the Blazers occupied with his tough defense while Terry Cummings led the way with 35 points in a gutsy 115-109 win.

David's coolness under pressure impressed Portland's head coach, Rick Adelman. "David's the most mature rookie I've ever seen," he said.

The Spurs battled all the way to a seventh and final game before the Blazers eliminated them. It was no disgrace.

Portland went on to the championship finals.

The 1989-90 season had been a dream come true for the people of San Antonio, who had waited out six stormy seasons for a winning team. Now the Spurs were winners again and they had drawn a team record 603,660 fans to their home games. The shipwrecked club had found its lucky red chameleon at last. His name was David Robinson.

"What's happened is that, in one season, this has become David's team," Coach Brown said. "He is its heart and soul. I'm not sure he even realizes that yet, because everything has happened so quickly. But the more he grows into that role, the better he'll become and the better the team will become."

David was already one step ahead of the coach. "A lot of people, just looking at my numbers, will say, 'He had a great year,'" David said. "But I look at myself every day and I see the things I need to work on, and I see I have so much farther to go."

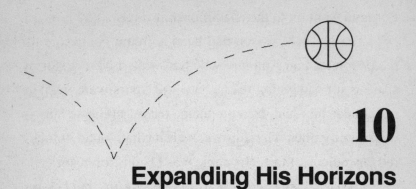

10

Expanding His Horizons

David Robinson is more than a talented athlete, a great basketball player, an intelligent man, and a special person. He is a unique sports superstar.

Most famous athletes achieve greatness only after years of practice that began in early childhood. David has never lived for basketball. He found greatness almost by accident.

"I never dreamed of being a pro in any sport," he says. "Basketball was just a shot in the dark. When you don't even like basketball as a freshman, it's hard to think of yourself playing full-time. I know a lot try out, and a lot don't make it. So few players make it through basketball. So few can be successful year in and year out."

The key to David's success is his willingness to learn and his ability to use his mind. "I'm a student at heart," he says. "I study great players like Terry Cummings, Michael Jordan, and Patrick Ewing, guys who play hard every night and have the heart to go with the talent. I ask myself, 'What makes them great?' There has to be something you can learn."

By keeping his mind open and not limiting his world to sports, David has learned many valuable lessons that help him on the basketball court. "I always want to expand my horizons," he says. "That's how I approach basketball."

David's parents taught him never to set limits on what he could achieve. "If you push yourself a little, you'll be surprised at what you can accomplish," he says. "I had to get pushed to achieve. My mother did the pushing. Where I'd be without her, I don't want to think about."

At the Naval Academy, David learned to be disciplined and confident. "The Naval Academy taught me to set goals and be persistent," he says. "If nothing else, I figured the Academy would get me a good job after graduation. I would have been happy if I hadn't made it in basketball. I feel I can do whatever I want with my life."

David was disappointed when the Navy made him wait two years to play pro basketball, but the experience taught him to be patient. "People I played with in college were out getting better and I wasn't," he says. "I didn't let it bother me, though, so I wasn't going to worry about it. I was going to enjoy being in the Navy."

Of course, life in the Navy wasn't always enjoyable. He was given important responsibilities at Kings Bay and lots of work. David learned to welcome challenges. "I love challenges, no matter what they are," he says. "I like people to expect a lot out of me. All I need to do is work hard. If I do that, everything will take care of itself."

David also learned in the Navy that he did not deserve special treatment simply because he was good at sports. "I got special treatment, but not the way you are thinking," he says. "They would really go out of their way to make things difficult for me just so people would know that I wasn't special."

Most of all, David learned how to be dedicated in everything he does. "Everything I've ever done in my life, when I saw I could be on top, I went after it," he says. "Now it's happening in basketball."

David has become a great basketball player by using the lessons he has learned. By not setting limits on what he can do, and by pushing himself, he will continue to improve. For example, during the 1989-90 season, David averaged 25.6 points, 13 rebounds, and 3.9 blocked shots per game. He also sank 55.2 percent of his field goals. After 32 games during the 1990-91 season, he was averaging 26.3 points, 12.9 rebounds, 4.56 blocks, and sinking 55 percent of his field goals.

"No matter how good I become, I'll never be satisfied with my game," he says. "There's always something more to do. When I retire, hopefully then I'll be satisfied."

By being disciplined and dedicated, he will make the most of his talent and skills. "I know you can't come here and do things halfway," he says. "The best players in the world are here, trying to beat you and trying to make you look bad. So I have to take this very seriously."

By being patient, David will give himself the time to gain the experience he needs to become a better player. Veteran players like his teammate, Terry Cummings, use their experience game after game. It has taught them not to get frustrated when they play poorly. They know how to make clutch plays when big games are on the line. They become familiar with opposing teams and how they play.

By welcoming challenges, David can face the best players in the league with confidence. "I don't give anybody respect unless they earn it," David says. "I saw Larry Bird, Patrick Ewing, Hakeem Olajuwon on TV and, yeah, they're good and everything. But until they come out on the court and play against me, that's when they start to earn their respect. I'm sure that's the way it is with everybody else when I come out on the floor. They're not going to give me anything until I perform."

By being humble, David will always be a team player. "I think any player would tell you that individual accomplishments help your ego, but if you don't win, it makes for a very, very long season. It counts more that the team has played well."

Bob Bass, the Spurs general manager, described David best when he said, "We've never had a center like him. He's just a terrific person."

"He has time for everyone," Coach Brown adds. "What's terrific is that he makes people feel good."

David feels good too. All his hard work, patience,

dedication, and eagerness to learn have brought him a great reward: a career in pro basketball. "I love it," he says. "I get up every morning and thank God because I have the best job in the world."

Of course, that job pays him millions of dollars, but that's not what David is about. "For those of us who play for the love of the game, money isn't a factor," he says. "Larry Bird and Michael Jordan are exactly what I'm talking about. You don't even think about how much they're making. You look at Michael Jordan and he should be the top-paid player in the league, all the things he does, the fans he brings in. Hopefully, I'll be able to do something similar to that. I'm not Michael Jordan, but I am David Robinson, you know."

Indeed he is, and you can bet he'll be doing big things for years to come. "He may go down as one of the greatest NBA players in history," says Marty Blake, the league's scouting director.

"Everything for me has turned out phenomenally," David says. "I couldn't ask for anything more. I just feel good about things, and I never want to lose perspective about what I have and where I'm going."

The sky's the limit, David.

David's NBA Statistics

1990-1991

Games	Rbs.	Assists	Steals	Blocks	Points	Avg.	High
82	1063	208	127	320	2101	25.6	43

1989-1990

Games	Rbs.	Assists	Steals	Blocks	Points	Avg.	High
82	983	164	257	319	1993	24.3	41

BASKETBALL COURT

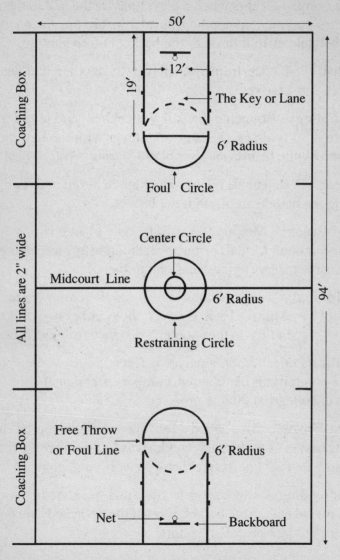

Glossary

Alley-oop: Occurs when a player passes the ball in the air toward the rim, and another player leaps in the air to catch the ball and slam it through the basket before landing.

Assist: A pass from one player to another that leads directly to a basket.

Dribbling: Bouncing the ball with either hand in order to move it up or down the court. A player with the ball must dribble while he moves.

Dunk: A shot made by jumping high in the air and slamming the ball down through the basket.

Fast Break: Moving the ball upcourt as fast as possible after a rebound, steal, or turnover in an effort to catch the defensive team off guard and outnumbered.

Field Goal: A successful shot from anywhere on the court, except a free throw. Field goals count as either two or three points, depending on the shooter's distance from the basket.

Fouling Out: When a player is forced to leave the game after committing his allotted number of personal fouls — five in college, six in the pros.

Free Throw: Also called a foul shot. An unhindered shot at the basket given to a player who was fouled. Thrown from behind the foul line, a free throw is worth one point.

Goaltending: Deflecting a shot that is already on its downward path to the basket. Even if the deflected shot does not go in, the basket still counts.

Hook Shot: Shot made while standing sideways to the basket and swinging the shooting arm around in a wide arc. The player releases the ball at the top of its arc.

Jump Shot: Shooter jumps in the air, and the ball is released from above the head at the top of the jump. It is the most popular shot in basketball.

Layup: A one-handed shot made from near or under the basket. The ball is usually banked off the backboard before it drops through the net.

Man-to-Man Defense: A style of defense in which each player is responsible for defending against a particular player on the other team.

Offensive Foul: A foul committed by a player when his team has possession of the ball.

Personal Foul: A foul involving illegal body contact between opposing players.

Rebound: Any missed shot that hits the backboard or rim and then bounces back toward the floor.

Traveling: Taking too many steps without a dribble while in possession of the ball. The team then loses the ball as a penalty.

Zone Defense: A style of defense in which players are responsible for defending a certain area of the court rather than a certain player on the other team.

About the Author

John Rolfe

John Rolfe has a Masters degree from the Columbia Graduate School of Journalism, and has worked as a reporter at *Sports Illustrated For Kids* since its first issue in January 1989. His articles have featured such sports stars as Mario Lemieux, Ron Darling and Brian Trottier. He has also written a book about sports trivia called *Curveballs: Wacky Facts to Bat Around*. Mr. Rolfe lives in North Babylon, Long Island with his wife Victoria, his sons Colin and Sean and their three cats.